You Can't Say You Can't Play

By the same author

White Teacher

Wally's Stories

Boys and Girls: Superheroes in the Doll Corner

Mollie Is Three: Growing Up in School

Bad Guys Don't Have Birthdays: Fantasy Play at Four

The Boy Who Would Be a Helicopter

You Can't Say  You Can't Play

Vivian Gussin Paley

Harvard University Press
Cambridge, Massachusetts, and London, England   1992

2513/301

This book is printed on acid-free paper, and its binding
materials have been chosen for strength and durability.

Library of Congress Cataloging-in-Publication Data

Paley, Vivian Gussin, 1929–
   You can't say you can't play / Vivian Gussin Paley.
      p. cm.
   ISBN 0-674-96589-2 (alk. paper)
   1. Kindergarten—Case studies. 2. Rejection
(Psychology) in children—Case studies. 3. Social
interaction in children—Case studies. 4. Play—Case
studies. 5. Teacher-student relationships—Case
studies. 6. Paley, Vivian Gussin, 1929– . I. Title.
LC1195.P183 1992
372.11'023—dc20   91-47700
                                        CIP

Designed by Gwen Frankfeldt

To

David and Elaine

Bobby and Jane

Contents

The stranger that sojourneth with you shall be unto you
as the homeborn among you, and thou shalt love him as thyself;
for you were strangers in the land of Egypt.

Leviticus 19:34

You Can't Play: The Habit of Rejection

Turning sixty, I am more aware of the voices of exclusion in the classroom. "You can't play" suddenly seems too overbearing and harsh, resounding like a slap from wall to wall. How casually one child determines the fate of another.

"Are you my friend?" the little ones ask in nursery school, not knowing. The responses are also questions. If yes, then what? And if I push you away, how does that feel?

By kindergarten, however, a structure begins to be revealed and will soon be carved in stone. Certain children will have the right to limit the social experiences of their classmates. Henceforth a ruling class will notify others of their acceptability, and the outsiders learn to anticipate the sting of rejection. Long after hitting and name-calling have been outlawed by the teachers, a more damaging phenomenon is allowed to take root, spreading like a weed from grade to grade.

Must it be so? This year I am compelled to find out. Posting a sign that reads YOU CAN'T SAY YOU CAN'T PLAY, I announce the new social order and, from the start, it is greeted with disbelief.

Only four out of twenty-five in my kindergarten class find the idea appealing, and they are the children most often rejected. The loudest in opposition are those who do the most rejecting. But everyone looks doubtful in the face of this unaccountable innovation.

What can I possibly mean, they wonder. Is there really to be unlimited social access into their private activities? What will happen to friendship? "But then what's the whole point of playing?" Lisa wails.

Fervently the children search for detours and loopholes as we debate the issues and, eventually, I bring the matter before the older students in the school. They too cannot imagine such a plan working. "You can't say you can't play?" It is very fair, they admit, but it just isn't human nature.

Fortunately, the human species does not live by debate alone. There is an alternate route, proceeding less directly, but often better able to reach the soul of a controversy. It is *story,* the children's preferred frame of reference. This time, however, *I* will be the storyteller, inventing Magpie, a bird who rescues those who are lonely or frightened and tells them stories to raise their spirits. I come to know Magpie well, for I will be the first one he saves.

The classroom seems all tumult and tears this year. My disapproval floats above us like a dark cloud, raining upon one child after another but mostly on me. I cannot locate the calm, rational center. And, besides, I think I am losing my voice.

It is with heavy spirits that I leave for a distant province in Canada to speak to some schoolteachers, ironically about happy classrooms. I'll be gone only two days but I feel I have abandoned those who need me and in so doing feel abandoned myself. Is Angelo fighting? Who comforts Clara when she hides in her cubby? I should not have left.

The trip is filled with long delays and discomfort, and no one meets me at the airport. After arriving at the hotel with barely time to change clothes, I enter the huge ballroom moments before my introduction. There is not a single person I know, and I cannot remember the names of the people who invited me. I feel a sense of panic. Who are these strangers, this blur of a thousand faces? Someone greets me as if I were an old friend and my anxiety increases, for I do not know the smiling face so close to mine. She starts to introduce me, speaking into the microphone, quoting from one of my books, but I cannot remember the words, and the voice that thanks her and begins to read my speech is breathless and unfamiliar. An hour later, I mumble excuses and leave quickly; in my loneliness I need to be alone.

The next morning I am in my running clothes before the sun is up. With the first glimmer of light, I begin my three-mile run in a deserted park across from the hotel. After four laps, which I estimate to be a mile, the empty feeling vanishes, as I knew it would. How often have I told the children "My running is like your play"? If I am sad, something mysterious happens when I run to make me feel good again, and thoughts come into my mind that help me figure things out. But now, the mystery is about to be revealed to me in an astonishing new way.

As I begin my second mile, a bird speaks to me. Yes, it

speaks to me. There is no doubt in my mind about it: In that misty Canadian dawn, a large black and white bird, one I have never seen before, calls to me each time I pass his tree. On my seventh lap, I whisper, "Who are you? Are you talking to me?" The bird moves to the tree ahead, and then to another, as if leading me on. Now the sun has cleared the lower branches and two women in white oxfords cross my path. "Excuse me," I say. "What kind of bird is that?" They laugh. "You really don't know? It's just a magpie." They continue on their way.

Ah, so you are a magpie. But do magpies not live in fairy tales? *A magpie flew by the tower of an ancient castle and heard the sound of crying. "Why do you cry, my lady?" he asked the sobbing princess. "I cry because I've been taken to this strange land and I am lonely for those I love. Can you help me, beautiful bird?" "Yes, I can. Climb on my back and we will fly twelve times around the castle walls. The spell will be broken and you will find yourself home again."*

The magpie's cawing startles me out of my fantasy and I laugh aloud. Suddenly I am in rhythm with the trees and the people and the buildings. I come upon a statue of Winston Churchill, and I feel the sting of tears. "Have you been here all along, Sir Winston?"

My spirit continues to soar as I shower, breakfast and, once again, mount a platform. Several hundred people are waiting with happy faces, and immediately I tell them the magpie story—there seems no way for me *not* to tell it—beginning with my feelings of the previous night. Someone in the audience gasps, pointing to the window in back of me, and I turn to see a magpie flying by. "So this is what it's like," I say. "This is how Angelo feels when he is a Ninja Turtle, in rhythm with the other turtles. He enters the classroom, into a land of strangers, and waits until he is caught up in a fantasy before he can see our smiles and smile back."

But then someone tells him he can't play and he sinks into gloom, adrift in a songless forest. *Magpie hovered over the castle tower . . . suddenly a child's sad voice drifted through the open window.*

Angelo turns away from me as I retell the story of the magpie in the park, but now he pushes through the others on the rug and drops at my feet. "Why was you watching that bird?" he demands.

"Is it a real bird?" Karl asks.

"The one in the park was real," I say, "but there is another one I call Magpie telling me stories in my mind."

The children are silent. Then Lisa says, "Oh, in your imagination."

"Why did you go away?" Angelo persists. "I had to tell you something and now I forgot."

"Maybe you'll remember . . ."

"No, I won't! It was a dream. And I don't like that Magpie you was watching."

Something is very strange down there, thought Magpie. He swooped through the treetops and circled the ancient castle walls. "I don't hear any birds!" he said. "Is it possible?"

Magpie was right. There were absolutely no birds in the forest below; not even the tap-tap-tap of a woodpecker could be heard. A forest without birds? This greatly disturbed the large black and white bird. It was like a lake without fish or a child without a friend.

Magpie hovered over the castle tower watching and listening for signs of life. Suddenly a child's sad voice drifted through an open window. The bird landed on the sill and peered into a small room lit by a single candle. Seated on a stone floor was a young girl slowly brushing her doll's hair.

"Pretend I'm your mother, little Maruska," the girl said, "and you thought I was dead. But then I came alive again and it's your birthday." A large tear traced a shiny path down the girl's cheek and splashed onto the doll's face. "Poor baby," sighed the girl. "Father will think you are crying too."

Magpie watched the child a moment longer. Her skin reminded him of the soft brown of a young robin and her hair of the black of a raven's tail. Where he came from the children were the color of the pale peaches that grew in Princess Alexandra's courtyard.

He gave a low whistle. "Excuse me, but are you in trouble? May I come in?"

The startled child hugged her doll in alarm and turned to the window. "Oh, a pretty bird!"

"My name is Magpie. Can I help you?"

"I don't think anyone can help me, Magpie. Since no one can bring my mother back to life, there is nothing to be done." The girl wrapped her doll in a large lacy shawl that trailed along the floor and then she stood up. "But you are welcome to come in. My father and I are very fond of birds."

How odd, thought Magpie. Fond of birds, yet they live in a place where there are none. "Is this your castle?" he asked.

The girl nodded. "I am Annabella and my father is Prince Kareem. We're descended from African kings and queens. Would you like to meet father? He spends a great amount of time studying birds."

This seemed even more curious to Magpie but he questioned the girl no further. "That's a very nice doll," he said, touching its shiny dress with his beak.

Annabella sat Maruska on Magpie's back and whispered, "Fly away, fly away, little one." Then she blushed. "I'm sorry, Magpie. Maruska and I are so lonely we've made you into a playmate. Does that seem strange?"

"Not at all," Magpie replied. He knew all about loneliness, for he had once been alone and lost while still in his shell. He also knew the way children play. "There is a girl in my kingdom named Princess Alexandra who talks to her doll as you do and sometimes she pretends I'm a giant who wants to steal it."

Annabella's eyes sparkled. "Oh, how I would like to play with Alexandra! But father says I must not wish for things I cannot have. Come, Magpie, follow me down the stairs. Father likes me to visit him at tea-time."

Before lunch, Angelo remembers his dream. "I was looking for my hamster and it was gone. Then my room was gone and then my house was gone but my grandma was there and she looks all around her and she doesn't see me."

"I have dreams like that," I tell him. "I'll be walking to school but the school isn't where it's supposed to be. Finally, I find the school on a different street and I go inside but none of the doors have my name on them. My dream is like yours."

Angelo seems surprised. "Then you and me is just the same, teacher." He smiles and touches my arm. His skin is the soft brown of a young robin, this restless child. When he stares at us his face is undecipherable, but he explodes with laughter if he is a superhero with other superheroes. And he knows how to make his dreams into stories.

"There was a boy and he was lost," he tells me later at the story table, where children dictate stories for us to act out on the piano rug. "And then he hears a noise and it's a hamster that was in a trap. Don't worry, I got the magic key. And the hamster turns into his brother because he forgot he had a brother."

Listening to the children's stories, I suddenly have a need to translate dreams into stories too, and my dreams tell me much about the loneliness of the outsider. My dreams and my memories. I can still recall the clouded faces of outcast children in the classrooms of my childhood, and also the faces of the confident ones who seemed to know exactly how everything must be done. They owned the secrets to life and it was important to me that I please and placate them.

It was important to the teachers also. We all fawned over the popular children and were impatient with the unchosen. "Popular" was good, "unpopular" was bad, and the unlikable ones were blamed for their faults.

My first grade teacher once said of an overweight girl,

"She'd have friends if she lost weight and changed her dress once in a while." I remember being shocked: *My* mother would never have said such a thing or allowed us to say it. Even so, I avoided that unlucky child and I was careful not to repeat the teacher's words at home.

From kindergarten on, I was not at ease in school, though I did well. To be accurate, I didn't really attend kindergarten. Miss Estelle, the teacher, advised my mother to take me out and keep me at home until first grade. "Your daughter just sits outside the circle and watches," she said. Much later, when I asked my mother why she didn't insist that I remain and learn how to enter the magic circle, she shrugged. "But that was the teacher telling me."

In any case, it did not take me long, in that first grade class, to know who was strong and who was weak and, except in dreams, I didn't side with the unloved. When I was older and came upon the biblical passage "The stranger that sojourneth with you shall be unto you as the homeborn among you . . ." I knew not that the first place a stranger sojourneth in is the classroom.

The little princess took the candle from the table and held her doll tightly as they started down the steep stairway. Magpie flew behind, lifting the shawl with his beak. When they came to the last turn in the stairs and could see the open door of the study, Annabella sat down abruptly. "Magpie," she whispered. "Before we go in, tell me about Alexandra. Does she look like a real princess?"

"As real as you, Annabella, though she is as light as you are dark. The two of you together are like my wing feathers." He spread his wings to show their colors and Annabella moved closer.

"Will you play something with me that you have played with Alexandra?" she asked.

"Of course," Magpie replied. *"Or, if you wish, I can tell you a story. That is something I also do with Alexandra."*

"Yes, a story! Mother used to tell me stories in the garden and all the birds would fly down to listen." The little girl's eyes grew moist and Magpie began his story quickly.

Once upon a time there was a lonely princess who wished every night upon the North Star that she might be a bird and fly away to find a playmate. Finally, one night, her wish was heard and she became a tiny yellow bird. "Follow me," the star called out. "When the first ray of sun dims my light you will see a fairy child waiting in the meadow below. You may play with her until the sun touches the top of the old oak tree. Then you must say goodbye and follow the last glimmer of my light back to your bed before your wings disappear."

For six nights the princess obeyed but on the seventh the play was so pleasant she forgot the warning. As the early morning dew began to sparkle in the sun, the girl saw she was no longer a bird. "Oh, dear," she moaned, "how shall I return to my father?" She wept and wept and soon all the fairies were crying with her. Their tears made a swiftly flowing river that carried the princess on a raft of lilies back to her kingdom.

When she awoke, the fairy child was beside her. "I'll stay and be your friend," said the fairy, "for you are the best playmate I've ever had."

Magpie lowered his head, pronouncing the story finished, and An-
nabella laughed with delight. Prince Kareem looked up from his desk
and called out, "Annabella, what has made you laugh? Come to me,
dear child. Tea is ready to be poured."

"We have a guest, father," Annabella said with a giggle. At this,
Magpie flew into the prince's study and landed on his desk.

"I am Magpie of the Kingdom of Tall Pines," he announced. "At
your service, sir."

The doctor calls my vocal problem "the teacher's curse" but
says it as if it is a badge of honor. He orders me to stop talking
so much, yet the more I try to limit myself the more I feel
compelled to speak.

"Something unhappy took place today in the blocks," I tell
the children at rug time. They sit close to me though my raspy
voice makes them uneasy. "I couldn't decide what to do about
Clara's unhappiness."

I have everyone's attention. Like me, they yearn for explanations of sadness. *"Magpie, is there such a thing as too many*
tears?" The children look at Clara to see if she is still sad. "A
lot of you," I continue, "think the teachers always know what
is right, but this time I don't think the fair thing was done.
You see, Clara was made to feel *unwanted. Not wanted.*"

Angelo looks at me the way he did when I spoke of going
to the doctor. He organizes himself quickly when the issue is
connected to feelings he recognizes—faster than I do. There

is an unrighted wrong here that I have avoided one way or another all of my years in the classroom. Do I hear the cry of lonely children more clearly because I myself am more vulnerable? I think of Clara and Angelo and know that they are being *rejected,* a word I seldom use in a classroom of young children. Surely the children are too innocent to understand the consequences of telling others they cannot play with them. Yet they reach out easily to those who are hurt or sad, often more tenderly than I. "Hurry up," they call to me. "Clara is crying!"

Shy Clara will speak for herself. "Cynthia and Lisa built a house for their puppies and I said can I play and they said no because I don't have a puppy only I have a kitty." This is the longest sentence she has spoken in school to date. There is more to come. "They said I'm not their friend." Clara hugs her tattered kitty and sniffs back her tears.

"We said if she brings a Pound Puppy she can play," Lisa explains.

Nelson frowns. "Ben wouldn't let me play."

"Uh-uh, it was Charlie, not me," Ben argues. "He was the boss."

"Me neither they wouldn't let me play," Angelo mutters. "Nobody that keeps worrying me like that I don't care about."

The children have warmed up to the subject. Being told you can't play is a serious matter. It hurts more than anything else that happens in school, and distractions no longer work very well. Everyone knows the sounds of rejection: You can't play; don't sit by me; stop following us; I don't want you for a partner; go away. These would be unforgivable insults if spoken at a faculty meeting, but our responses are uncertain in the classroom.

Even the victim does not know how to react. "I'll tell my mommy if she could get me that kind of puppy like they have," Clara offers.

"They has to let her play," Sheila insists. "Unless they really don't want to."

"Unless she really really can't find someone else to play with," Cynthia adds, looking guiltily at Lisa.

Their ambivalence and mine are similar. "It's a hard problem," I agree, "and the same thing happens to other children *every day.*"

"To me," Angelo says.

"Me too," adds Nelson.

"And me." It is Smita. I hadn't realized Smita was having these problems. *The rejected children know who they are,* whether or not they tell us.

"When it happens to Clara she cries and sits in her cubby," I say. "I found her there and we went to see the girls. Lisa said she didn't want anyone else, that they didn't need another person. But I said, 'Clara needs you even if you think you don't need her.'"

Cynthia lowers her eyes. "I wanted her to play."

"But it was my game!" Lisa cries. "It's up to me!" She is red-faced and tearful. "Okay, I won't play then, ever!"

The children watch the participants in the drama. My voice is barely audible as I continue the narrative. "So, I thought, I want to do a favor for Clara, but is it fair to spoil Lisa's and Cynthia's play? Yet would this really spoil their play? How?

Well, I couldn't figure out what to do. Luckily, Mary Louise came along and agreed to play with Clara."

It hurts when I try to clear my throat and I sip slowly on the water I keep with me all the time now. The doctor's specific advice was: Don't project your voice, and drink a lot of water. "I just can't get the question out of my mind," I say softly. "Is it fair for children *in school* to keep another child out of play? After all, this classroom belongs to all of us. It is not a private place, like our homes."

"Like that place where Magpie lives at," Angelo says.

"The Kingdom of Tall Pines?" I am startled and moved by Angelo's reference to Magpie. Throughout the year, whenever the children speak to me of Magpie it is as if they speak to me of love.

"Yeah, in that place everyone can play—that right, teacher?"

"I hope so." But I am not certain. *"You were not afraid to live in a strange place, Magpie?"*

I have a new Magpie chapter ready but my voice is not up to the task of reading aloud. These days I am up before dawn drinking hot tea with honey and working on the Magpie stories. Luckily, my assistant, Sarah Wilson, knows my handwriting even when it has been hurriedly entered into my journal.

Now, as I sit silently outside the circle of faces, I am lonely, as if I've been told I can't play. I wonder if this is the way I felt as a kindergartener when I was afraid to enter the group.

Prince Kareem pushed back his chair in surprise and stared at the unexpected guest on his desk. "Magpie? Magpie? Just one moment, please." He reached for a heavy book and rapidly turned the pages. "J, K, L, M . . . ah, here it is. 'Magpie: yellow-billed magpie, has iridescent black plumage, white wing patches and abdomen, and a long graduated tail. It collects colorful objects and can imitate words and the sounds of birds.'"

He closed the book and smiled. "Well, this encyclopedia doesn't know the whole of it. You speak as well as I do. And, do you collect colorful objects? Forgive me for being so nosy but, you see, birds are my hobby. I'm writing a book about them."

Magpie was pleased. "Then you are a storyteller as I am."

Princess Annabella sat on her father's lap and smiled up at him. "But father writes of true things, Magpie, and your stories are only pretend," she said.

"Dear Annabella," Magpie replied modestly, "my stories are no less true than those contained in these piles of books. The story I just told you of the lonely princess who wished to be a bird is as real in your mind as all your other thoughts."

"Quite right, Magpie," the prince agreed. "We each tell our stories in different ways. Perhaps the reason I write about birds and draw their pictures is that I too would like to be a bird and fly away."

Magpie fluttered about the room examining the drawings on the walls. "These birds of yours look as if they could soar up to the sky in an instant." He returned to the desk and watched Annabella pour tea into large mugs for him and her father and into tiny dolls' cups for herself and Maruska. Then he turned to the prince and hopped closer. "May I ask a personal question, Prince Kareem?"

"Certainly," said the prince, stirring his tea. "Ask anything you wish."

"Well, then, plainly put, how is it that you and Annabella, who both love birds and children, live in a place where there are none?"

The dark, gray-haired man gently patted his daughter's arm and gazed out the window. "This was a very different place when my wife was alive. Her beautiful singing attracted birds and people from many lands. These woods were filled with song and laughter." The prince touched a handkerchief to his eyes.

Annabella kissed her father's cheek and continued the story. "After mother died the birds flew away, one by one, and soon the people moved away too. Magpie, is there such a thing as too many tears?"

My voice has improved only a little but I have a speaking commitment in Arizona that cannot be canceled. This will definitely be my last trip until the hoarseness clears up. Before I leave, the children and I talk again about the question that persists in my mind. I tape the discussion in order to listen to it on the plane. The replay of children's voices often helps clarify a problem for me. I cannot hear everything the first time around.

Teacher: Should one child be allowed to keep another child from joining a group? A good rule might be: "You can't say you can't play."

Ben: If you cry people should let you in.

Teacher: What if someone is not crying but feels sad? Should the teacher force children to say yes?

Many voices: No, no.

Sheila: If they don't want you to play they should just go their own way and you should say, "Clara, let's find someone who likes you better."

Angelo: Lisa and her should let Clara in because they like Clara sometimes but not all the time so they should let her in.

Nelson: They don't play with her too much so they should let her in.

Teacher: Angelo and Nelson think that even if you don't like someone all the time or play with her very much, she should have a chance to play. Shall we insist upon it? . . . I can see you don't think so.

Charlie: If I was playing, I'd let Clara in.

Teacher: When you play with Ben do you always let others in?

Charlie: Not if it's too special I might not.

Ben: Like when we was Transformers and Nelson he wanted to come in—he always has to, that's the problem—but we couldn't stop playing so I said Charlie has to decide because I didn't care and he was the boss.

Nelson: Both people can decide.

Angelo: They always like someone else better.

Waka: I say let two people whoever wants to play. But who they don't want has to find someone else. My brother says that. He's in fourth grade.

Teacher: We should ask the older children about this.

Angelo: Let anybody play if someone asks.

Lisa: But then what's the whole point of playing?

Nelson: You just want Cynthia.

Lisa: I could play alone. Why can't Clara play alone?

Angelo: I think that's pretty sad. People that is alone they has water in their eyes.

Lisa: I'm more sad if someone comes that I don't want to play with.

Teacher: Who is sadder, the one who isn't allowed to play or the one who has to play with someone he or she doesn't want to play with?

Clara: It's more sadder if you can't play.

Lisa: The other one is the same sadder.

Angelo: It has to be Clara because she puts herself away in her cubby. And Lisa can still play every time.

Lisa: I can't play every time if I'm sad.

How clearly the issue is stated. Later, when I read this part of the transcript to some older children, they all agree with Angelo and Clara. However, in practice, they admit, they follow the course set by Lisa.

No one wants to force the issue. And so Clara will continue to find solace in her cubby and Angelo will stare at us as if we are strangers. Furthermore, Charlie will get used to being the boss and Lisa can push Clara out one day and Smita the next and Cynthia after that. The way we do it, exclusion is written into the game of play. And play, as we know, will soon be the game of life.

Listening to the tape on the plane, I hear Lisa's plaintive "But then what's the whole point of playing?" and Nelson's knowing response, "You just want Cynthia." Is the primary purpose of play to have and to hold a best friend? Or to establish who's the boss? If, indeed, possessiveness comes first, then how can any plan work that attempts to eradicate exclusive ownership?

The next morning at sunrise, as I run past tall cactus plants tipped in orange flowers, I try to pin down a few premises. First of all, play, in and of itself, gives pleasure. It is certainly attached to friendship but the equation is a tricky one. Play flows out of friendship and friendship flows out of play. The relationship works both ways and equally well, but the children are not convinced that this is so, a suspicion that grows stronger as they grow older.

The children I teach are just emerging from life's deep wells of private perspective: babyhood and family. Possessiveness and jealousy are inescapable concomitants of both conditions. Then, along comes school. It is the first real exposure to the public arena. Children are required to share materials and teachers in a space that belongs to everyone. Within this public space a new concept of open access can develop if we choose to make this a goal. Here will be found not only the strong ties of intimate friendship but, in addition, the habit of full and equal participation, upon request.

Equal participation is, of course, the cornerstone of most classrooms. This notion usually involves everything *except* free play, which is generally considered a private matter. Yet, in truth, free acceptance in play, partnerships, and teams is what matters most to any child.

We vote about nearly everything in our democratic classrooms, but we permit the children to empower bosses and reject classmates. Just when the old-fashioned city bosses have all but disappeared and the once exclusive dining clubs are opening their doors to strangers, we still allow children to build domains of exclusivity in classrooms and playgrounds.

"In your whole life you're not going to go through life never being excluded," a fifth grade boy will tell me. "So you may as well learn it now."

"Maybe our classrooms can be nicer than the outside world," I suggest.

"But then," he argues, "you won't be so down on yourself when you do get excluded."

I don't give up. He looks as if he has known rejection. "Here's what troubles me, as a teacher," I tell the fifth graders. "Too often, the same children are rejected year after year. The burden of being rejected falls on a few children. They are made to feel like strangers."

Magpie thought about the sad tale he had just heard. Who can say when tears are too many? "I can't answer that question," he said, "but I can offer my own story in return for yours. Would you like to hear how a witch named Beatrix saved my life?"

The prince and Annabella became very quiet and Magpie began. "Well, then, for reasons unknown, one day, just as I was starting to peck out of my shell, I found myself lost, alone, and partly buried in a clump of moss and pine needles under a tall pine tree. I kept pecking, of course, for once you begin you cannot stop. It is exhausting work, believe me.

"Then, during a moment's pause, I heard loud angry voices above me. There stood two girls, a bit older than you, Annabella, arguing and pushing each other. I saw them clearly through the tiny opening in my shell. I didn't know at first that they were sisters and, besides that, witches, but I soon discovered it was me they were fighting about.

"Sylvia was about to step on me but Beatrix screamed at her not to touch me, that I was a magpie egg. Oh, how they pushed and quarreled. It's a wonder I didn't get smashed. Sylvia kept coming back and holding her foot over me; I could actually see the bottom of her shoe."

Annabella covered her face with her hands. "Oh, Magpie, how awful! You must have been so frightened."

Magpie nodded. "I was frozen with fear. I can remember it all as if it were happening right now. I remember Beatrix explaining that magpies are special birds, birds of joy, but her sister wasn't curious in the least about this information."

"Is it true, Magpie?" the prince asked. "The encyclopedia doesn't mention that."

"Well, Beatrix believed it was true. 'Keep away, little sister,' she warned. 'I'm taking care of this poor orphan and that's final!' Sylvia stomped off and Beatrix began to make a nest for me. She knew how a magpie nest looks, a bit like a thatched cottage."

Annabella was puzzled. "Magpie, why was Beatrix so nice to you? Aren't witches usually bad?"

"Beatrix says she's not a proper witch," he replied. "Not mean *enough. Oh, she can be naughty, all right, especially when she's jealous, but mostly she wants to play just as you do. Her sisters are more like real witches. They wouldn't have protected me as Beatrix did. She raised me as her own child. And so, even though there were no other magpies around, I decided to stay. Her home, the Kingdom of Tall Pines, became my home."*

Prince Kareem had begun to draw Magpie's picture on a large piece of paper. His chalks moved quickly, covering the sheet with colors and lines that soon became Magpie's head and then his tail. When the sketch was completed the prince taped it to the wall between his drawings of an eagle and a robin. Then he returned to his chair to watch Annabella and Magpie play hide-and-seek around the table.

After a while, Prince Kareem spoke. "You were not afraid to live in a strange place, Magpie? Do you think Annabella and I would be happy there too among the tall pines? We would be strangers."

Annabella's eyes opened wide. Would her father really be willing to leave their castle and go to a new land? "We wouldn't be strangers, father!" she exclaimed. "We already know Magpie and I know some things about Princess Alexandra. Oh, and don't forget Beatrix!"

Magpie flew around the room excitedly, then perched on the highest pile of books. "There are fourteen children who live in the Kingdom of Tall Pines," he stated, "and they all go to a little schoolhouse. There are dozens of varieties of birds; I myself have counted seven kinds of woodpeckers. Oh, and there is even a thatched cottage no one lives in!"

The prince stood up and took his daughter's hand. "Well, my friend," he said to Magpie, "perhaps you were sent to us by some

*magical force. I believe such things can happen. Will you tell us how
to travel to your kingdom?"*

*Magpie flapped his wings and whistled. "I'll do better than that,
Prince. Pack up your carriage and I'll lead the way!"*

*There are fourteen children who live in the Kingdom of Tall Pines
and they all go to a little schoolhouse.*

Ah, bliss. How do they get along at the sand table, I wonder.
Ours is impossible today. Everyone seems determined to ruin
someone else's play and I have little desire to sort out the
messy details. Nothing would suit me better than just to cover
the table.

*A huge eagle came swooping down upon the orange flowers, caus-
ing them to tumble down the mountainside . . .*

"Why not divide the sand into separate sections and play
alone?" I urge hoarsely. "There's too much arguing. I can't
hear the stories."

"Angelo started it," Charlie says.

"They was fixin' to steal my sand," Angelo snaps angrily,
"from my hill. Anyway, they's too nasty. I'm leaving!"

Wiping his hands on his pants, he makes a sand trail to the
story table. Then, wearily, he puts down his head, closing his
eyes. A moment later he springs up. "Can I tell a story,
teacher?"

"Good," I say, taking his notebook from the pile. "I'm in the
mood for a story." The moment he begins a calm descends

over this table, though the sand players are still noisy and quarrelsome at theirs.

"Some men was hunting in the forest. They saw something up in the hill and they started climbing. And they was climbing until they got to the top and it was a baby fox was trapped and they was trying to get the baby fox out. It was crying for its mother. Don't worry, fox, we'll take you home and start you a fire. They was trying to help him, not to hurt him. They took him home and the mother fox was there. And the baby said, 'I thought you was dead.' And the hunter said, 'She come alive.' And they started a fire to keep warm."

Clara also wants to tell a story. "There was a little kitty. And there was a little girl. And the girl's name is Lisa and the kitty's name is Clara and they live together."

For years I have written down these stories the children invent, the fairy tales of the young. Their voices have seeped into my consciousness and become as my own. What if I were to say, "I don't want your story, Angelo. I'll find someone I like better, Clara, to tell me a story"? It could never happen, of course. Yet I allow the children to do this at play.

"I asked those Arizona teachers what they do when one child tells another child he can't play." The children are already curious about my trip to Arizona because I've told them that a new Magpie story came into my mind while I looked at the big cactus plants covered with orange flowers.

"What do the teachers do?" several children ask.

"First they try to convince the children to be kind and let one another play. But if that doesn't work, they help the one who is rejected find another playmate, just as we do."

The children have learned "rejected." No euphemism will do. Rejection in play is the forerunner of all the rejections to come. Of course, the feeling begins much earlier, in life's first separations. We are so vulnerable once we are alone at school.

"Some of the Arizona teachers think it's probably best to just let children figure out these problems for themselves."

"What do we figure out for ourself?" Charlie asks me.

"Your play and your stories. I don't say what they must be about."

"You don't tell us what to paint," Smita says, "but Jennifer always tells me."

"She likes to give people advice," I say, "but you don't always do what she tells you, right?"

Angelo wants to know what else I *don't* tell the children. "I try not to tell you what thoughts or opinions to have," is my less than honest answer, at a time when I am single-mindedly pushing new attitudes about play.

"We have to come to the rug . . ."

"And come to a discussion . . ."

"But I don't tell you what to *say* in the discussion," I hasten to point out. "And I listen to everyone."

"We have to take turns to talk."

This is the first time the children examine my role with such intensity. Is it that they sense I am about to change something in a way they may not like? Do I have this right, or even the obligation to enforce free access in the face of their strong feelings of self-determination?

"Anyway, here is what else I said to those teachers. That I am certain the children who are told they can't play don't learn as well. They might become too sad to pay attention."

"Is Clara too sad to pay attention?" Cynthia asks.

"Not yet. But we don't want it to happen, to Clara or to anyone else. We don't want anyone to feel as sad as Prince Orange Flower when he is trapped in the eagle's nest."

"Who is he?"

"You'll see. He's in the story I made up when I was in Arizona."

"What else don't you tell us?" persists Clara. It is unusual for her to push beyond what the others seek to know. "I don't say: *Let* Clara play in your house, just because she wants to play there."

Her eyes open wide as if she is about to hear a secret. "But I think I should tell that to everyone, Clara. What do you think?"

"Yes," she replies in a loud voice.

He knew all about loneliness for he had once been alone and lost while still in his shell.

"First I want to talk to the older boys and girls. When we return from spring vacation I'll visit the first, second, third, fourth, and fifth grades." The children like hearing the litany of grade numbers. Even those with older siblings in those classes feel a sense of awe when contemplating being in a grade with a number. "We'll find out what the big children think of 'You can't say you can't play.'"

The prince and Annabella soon filled two large trunks, one with clothing and dolls and the other with books and journals. "I'd rather get out and walk than leave a single book behind," he told Annabella as he harnessed the horses. Then he gave Magpie chalk and paper and asked him to draw a map.

"Yes, a ground map is essential," Magpie said, "though mine won't be too accurate. I know the route only as a bird flies." Magpie walked back and forth across the paper, then picked up a chalk in his beak and marked an X in the upper left-hand corner.

"This X is where we are. Over here is where we want to go." He printed another X on the other side, halfway down, then raised himself a few inches off the ground and flew between the X's. "Ah, much better. I remember it quite well now." He began to draw a line, first very straight, then curvy, and finally as wavy as the ocean.

"There. The straight road takes us along the edge of the Great Desert, no more than a day's ride. Then we'll be on a winding trail that passes through some high mountains. I always count the peaks when I fly over them." Magpie took a piece of white chalk and drew six snow-capped tips. Farther over, he covered the wavy lines with blue chalk.

"This water is the Silver Sea. We'll have to wait for a boat to carry us across, but at this point our journey is nearly over. On the opposite shore is a pine forest so thick it looks like a solid wall. That is the entrance to the Kingdom of Tall Pines."

"Let me draw the trees, Magpie," Annabella said, taking up pieces of brown and green chalk. In a moment, the second X was surrounded by tall trees.

The prince rolled up the map and gave his castle one last look. "Giddap!" he shouted, shaking the reins. "On our way! Yup! Yup!"

He and Annabella were soon deep in thought as they left the silent forest and rode through the hilly meadows beyond. But when they reached the Great Desert their mood suddenly brightened. To their surprise, the road was lined with huge flowering cactus plants. They looked like giants holding orange and purple flowers in outstretched arms. "Oh, can we stop, please, father?" Annabella begged. "I want to smell the flowers."

The carriage came to a halt and Annabella jumped out. "I think I'll make a few sketches," the prince said. "Magpie, we've never seen the desert before. The shapes and colors are astonishing. Annabella, dear, would you pick me a flower of each color, please, so I can copy its exact shade later?"

But the moment the little princess reached for an orange flower, its petals snapped shut. She tried another, careful to avoid the sharp thorns, but it too closed instantly, and she was certain she could hear whispers coming from inside the blossoms.

The Inquiry: Is It Fair?
Will It Work?

After spring vacation, I organize a schedule of discussions with the older students. A week of silence and endless cups of tea have produced a noticeable improvement in my voice and I am eager to expose "You can't say you can't play" to public scrutiny.

The teachers are cooperative and curious. They are quite used to my passionate espousals, and this is a problem about which there is widespread concern. In general, the approach has been to help the outsiders develop the characteristics that will make them more acceptable to the insiders. I am suggesting something different: The *group* must change its attitudes and expectations toward those who, for whatever reason, are not yet part of the system.

The response of the first grade children surprises me in its intensity. Indeed, as I proceed through the Lower School, each grade level will reveal a markedly different approach to the subject, but high emotion will govern them all.

Following a brief introduction, I pose two questions: Is the new rule fair? Can it work? A barrage of memories is unleashed. The children, it would seem, have not forgotten a single rejection to which they may have been subjected during the previous kindergarten year. Each incident is recalled with clarity, as if it just happened. Several children had been in my own class and they describe in detail events unknown to me at the time or certainly forgotten by now.

"This is what happened to me," a girl says. "Two girls had a certain kind of doll and they wouldn't let me play because I didn't have that doll."

"That's like these guys, a lot of time they said I couldn't play," a boy tells us, "but then someone came they like better than me and they let him play."

The subject of rejection touches a universal sensitivity. "There's this game we play and then one person, the one who's the boss, always says he's the good guy and I have to be a robber or I can't play."

"How does someone get to be the boss?" I ask.

"If you start the game . . ."

"Because you say it . . . you know how it's supposed to go."

"People just let you . . . because someone has to be the one who tells everyone."

The girl who didn't have the special doll in kindergarten disagrees. "What if the girl who made up that game doesn't like that other girl and the other girl says, yeah, let's let her play, and the other girl who made up the game says no. Then the other girl can say yes."

I repeat her statement. "So, *besides* the one who made up the game, the others can say 'Let this person play.'" The question of shared responsibility for social decisions will remain a sticky point in every grade.

"Yeah," a boy responds, "but what if someone lets somebody who is their best friend play, then here comes your worst friend, then he says can I play and she says yes and the other one says no?" The boy who has just spoken looks around, wanting support. These children don't need me to connect their thoughts, not when the subject is so vividly, even painfully, personal.

"That's right! And then *your* best friend leaves! See, it won't work. It'll just make people mad."

"Here's what happened to me," a girl says, looking across the rug at a classmate. "This person who didn't make up the game said I could play and then we start playing and then the one who did make up the game tried to get me out."

"Because we already had everyone we needed," the girl she is looking at explains.

"That wasn't fair," says the boy next to her. "If someone is already in a game, you should be able to stay."

A boy who had been in my class tells me, "It's hard for that rule you made up to work because, see, there could be more fights, not less fights. See, if someone says you can't play and then there is a rule, so they begin to fight about the rule."

"And if there's no rule?" I ask.

"Then the person just walks away. That's better."

"But I don't understand the rule," a girl complains. "Like what if I only want two sisters and then more people come and more people and more and it's so confusing."

"That would be confusing," I admit. "Has this ever happened, where so many children wanted to play in your game?"

"No," she answers simply. "But what if it was someone mean you didn't like?"

There is a moment of silence while we all contemplate the

intrusion of strange and unwanted people into our intimate games. During the pause I tell the children a true story. "Some of you know Mrs. Wilson, who teaches with me. Her building shares a backyard with two other buildings. All the children in all the buildings play in that one yard and they follow a simple rule: *Everyone can play.* When a child comes out the older ones ask, 'Do you want to play?' And if someone is mean or fights a lot they tell him or her not to do it and they keep saying it until the child remembers to play nicely."

The children are fascinated by my story. "What do you think of Mrs. Wilson's backyard?" I ask.

"It's very nice."

"Those are really nice kids."

"I wish I lived there."

"So do I," I say. "Could this happen in a classroom?"

"Maybe," says the boy who worried about my rule causing more fighting. "It's very fair. But people aren't that fair as the rule is."

"Anyway, I think it *is* fair if girls want to play alone," a girl says softly.

"Or boys can play alone," adds the boy next to her.

"But what if a girl is curious?" I ask the boy. "Let's say she has no brothers and she wants to know more about boys. Or what if a boy is curious about the way girls play?"

His answer satisfies everyone: "Ask the girl if she has a brother and if she says no she can play. And if it's a boy with no sisters then the girls should let him play. That would be fair."

The prince frowned when he heard what had happened. "You did well to leave the flowers alone, Annabella. Clearly they do not wish to be touched. Don't you agree, Magpie?"

"Absolutely. Every living thing knows its own dangers. And, prince, speaking of dangers, the desert grows cold at night. I suggest you complete your drawings quickly so we can arrive at the mountain pass before dark. We'll want to find a cave for the night."

Prince Kareem replaced the chalks and signaled the horses to move on. Now the travelers kept up a steady pace until the mountain range rose up before them. The sun was beginning to disappear behind the jagged cliffs when the carriage reached a sharp turn in the road. "I believe we should stop here," the prince said, pointing to a nearby cave. He tied the horses to a tree. Then he filled his arms with blankets and pillows, and his chalk box and drawing pad. Annabella carried Maruska and the food basket.

Magpie had already begun to bring moss into the cave. "See if you can reach those piles of soft grasses over there," he called. "You'll need a large nest in here if you are to rest comfortably."

Annabella wrapped her doll in its shawl and placed it in a circle of moss. "Sleep well, little baby," she whispered. "You'll soon be in your new home."

Then she went out to help collect the bedding. She spied a cluster of flowers on a ledge above and began to climb up to them. Suddenly she called out, "Father! Magpie! Look up there! Aren't those the same orange desert flowers? I can see them moving!"

Before the prince or Magpie could reply, a huge eagle came swoop-

ing down upon the orange flowers, causing them to tumble down the mountainside—all but one, the smallest, which was lifted by the eagle into the air and taken to a nest on a cliff high above them.

"A golden eagle!" the prince exclaimed. "Why would it pounce that way on a bunch of flowers? And how can flowers move about so?"

Magpie stretched his wings to their full width. "I'll fly up and investigate," he said, but Annabella scrambled up in front of him.

"I'm coming too, Magpie," she shouted. "These rocks are no harder to climb than our trees at home."

"For me they would be," the prince admitted. "I'll stay and feed the horses. Do be careful, Annabella."

Magpie flew nervously alongside Annabella. Her arms and legs did not seem as reliable as wings. Whenever Beatrix needed to leave the ground she turned herself into a brown moth, but Annabella couldn't do that, of course, because she was not a witch. "Magpie, look, the flowers are waving to us," the little girl cried.

"They're not flowers at all!" Magpie exclaimed. "They're tiny little people! And they're dressed in those orange petals you tried to pick in the desert. That eagle has stolen a tiny child!"

Magpie called up to the frightened flower people beginning to reassemble on the rocks above. "Hello, there! I'm Magpie and this is Princess Annabella. We saw what just happened. Can we be of any help?"

"My story got a eagle in it too," Angelo tells me, settling down at the story table. "Not for kidnapping or nothing like that. My eagle is a good guy. He was taking me to the North Pole. Then some men was trying to shoot him. And they couldn't so they told the boss and he stretched out his slingshot real far and he hit the wing and the eagle said 'Auk! Auk!' And then we flew away and when we was at the North Pole I fixed the eagle's wing."

Nelson slumps down next to Angelo. "Those guys won't let me play," he complains, watching me finish writing down Angelo's story.

"They just wanna be alone by their own self," Angelo comments.

"They're making me to be a bad Transformer." Nelson is discouraged. Everyone knows Nelson never wants to be a bad guy. Telling him he must take that role effectively shuts him out. Charlie and Ben have the power to do this. The boss can stretch out his slingshot and shoot down anyone. My job seems to be to fix the eagle's wing after it is hit.

I call Charlie and Ben over and read Angelo's story to them. "When you tell Nelson he must be the bad guy, it's like the boss hitting the eagle's wing."

"We told him *nicely* he could play because we need a bad guy. We started the game."

"I know, and that makes you think you own the game. It doesn't seem fair. Can't there be three good-guy Transformers?"

Ben answers patiently and sincerely. "See, we're not playing that there is."

Later, when they let Karl be the third good guy, I am indignant. "You cannot do this, boys. It is absolutely not fair to Nelson." Karl is confused and hurt. He scowls at me, and he is right to be angry. Mine is as arbitrary an infliction of pain on Karl as the boys imposed on Nelson.

The trouble is, there is no dependable rule that protects everyone equally from the slings and arrows of boss rule. Even Clara is capable of rejecting someone. After lunch, she and Lisa tell Cynthia she can't play. Why would Clara take part in this manipulative act, knowing how it feels? When I point this out to her she looks away but is not inclined to give up her sudden and unexpected good fortune. Her wish has come true. Lisa has chosen to play with her today, a temporary whim that will make the next rejection all the more puzzling and painful.

"They won't let me be a mousie sister," Cynthia protests. She has been offered the role of a friend who lives next door which, of course, is not as good as being a sister living in the same house.

Nearby at the sand table, Waka is crying because Angelo either pushed or hit him, it is hard to tell. "He messed up my road on purpose!" Angelo yells. "Just 'cause they don't want me to play!"

"But look at Waka, Angelo. You made him cry." My forced whisper sounds angrier than Angelo's outburst. "Don't *ever* push or hit, Angelo. I've told you that." There is no ambivalence on my part nor any attempt to persuade. He runs to his cubby and suddenly I remember that Angelo never tells children they cannot play.

Before we go home, I flip through my notebook until I come to a page with FIRST GRADE printed at the top. Everyone wants to see the title so I hold up the page and then read the numbered list of points made by the first graders:

1. Maybe the rule will cause fighting.
2. Maybe too many people will want to play.
3. Maybe someone will be mean to you.
4. Is it fair to tell someone he has to be a robber?
5. If you say no to one person, can you say yes to someone else?
6. If the owner says no, can another player still say yes?
7. Girls should be allowed to say only girls can play and boys should be allowed to say only boys can play. Unless they're very curious about each other's play.

The children stare at me and at the list in amazement. To think that *our* subject is worthy of such a response! Of course, except for the boy-girl part, we have debated every topic on the list among ourselves. However, it is an entirely different experience to realize that what we talk about is of enormous interest to others and that their ideas sound so familiar.

I end with a personal note: "What interested me most is that even though the children thought it would be hard for our plan to work, they all remembered what happened to them when they were in kindergarten, especially the bad things."

"What were the bad things?" Lisa asks.

"When someone wouldn't let them play."

Magpie watched Annabella scamper up the rocky path. She's like a mountain goat, he thought. By the time the tiny flower people had

gathered together again, the princess was seated nearby, examining them closely. Their clothing, including hats and shoes, was stitched from flower petals and their skin was the color of the desert sand. "Do you live inside the orange cactus flowers?" Annabella asked. "I thought I heard voices when I tried to pick them."

"Yes, that is exactly where we live," answered an excited woman wearing an orange crown. "I am Queen Orangelina. That terrible monster of an eagle has taken my son, Prince Orange Flower. But why? We often come up here to sip from these icy streams and it's never been a dangerous place."

The queen burst into tears and the others ran to her with words of comfort. "It's not your fault, my queen," said an elderly man. "These mountains have always been safe. It is only the unlucky seventh mountain we are forbidden to climb."

"The seventh?" Magpie asked in surprise. "But I count only six peaks when I fly over these mountains."

"You cannot see the seventh mountain because it is covered by clouds and fog," the man explained. "But we know that dragons live there. Our grandparents have seen their footprints and heard their fiery roars." He sat down and began to weep. "Now we'll have to stop coming here also."

Magpie spoke to the queen. "Your Highness, I doubt if the eagle intends to harm your son. Eagles do not attack people. He was probably curious about your bright colors and your movements. However, the little prince must be returned to you. I shall see to that."

The queen wiped her eyes and stared up at Magpie. "You would do battle with such a giant bird?"

Magpie shook his head. "Not a battle," he said. "I have learned from a friend who is a witch that trickery can be more useful than sheer power."

The tiny people nodded. "We know all about trickery," said a gentleman who introduced himself as Uncle Orangerio. "When you are as small as we are that is often the best defense."

"Tricks such as locking your petals?" asked Annabella. "And disguising yourselves as flowers?"

A little child pulled himself onto Annabella's lap and stood on tiptoe. "We make buzzing noises," he whispered, "and we squirt out something that stings, and we cover the thorns so the enemy won't see them until it's too late, and . . ."

Annabella clapped her hands. "Those are wonderful tricks," she said, "but who are your enemies?"

The child looked surprised. "Don't you know those lizards who steal our sweet nectar, and the big people who want to pick us?"

Annabella blushed. "Oh, dear! I just tried to do that," she admitted. "But I promise never to be your enemy again."

Everyone turned to look at Magpie, who had flown to a rock above them and was pacing back and forth. "I've thought of a plan," he called out, "but unfortunately it requires two of us to make it work!"

"I'll come!" Annabella shouted. "Now that I've rested you'll see how fast I can climb."

Uncle Orangerio jumped up and ran to the edge. "Let me come, too, Magpie. I know these rocks. I can warn Annabella about the loose ones."

Magpie fluttered his tail feathers. "I'm afraid neither of you could reach the nest in the dark, and my plan will work only in the dark." He continued pacing. Each time he came to the edge of the cliff he flew

*out in another direction and squinted up at the eagle's nest high
above them. The darkening sky was streaked with red and the
mountain peaks were beginning to fade from view. "Annabella," he
called, "you must return to your father. Soon you'll not be able to
see where you're climbing."*

The second graders put away their books the moment they
see me and move to the edges of the rug. "I've come to ask
your opinions about a new rule we're considering in the
kindergarten. It says you can't exclude people, you can't reject
them. We call it 'You can't say you can't play.'"

The children need no further introduction; they know the
territory well. "My sister says she won't play with me and I
say okay then I'll play by myself and I can be whatever I
want."

"That's like my big brother," a boy says. "I ask can I play
and he always says no and my mom tells us work it out."

"Perhaps those are good solutions at home," I comment,
"but what about when it happens in school?"

"Just play with someone else . . . but if my friend is playing
that game I just go somewhere else."

"Naw you don't," mutters the boy next to him. "He goes to
the teacher."

"Is that wrong?" I ask.

"It's okay but I'm just saying he doesn't just go somewhere
else."

"How about you?" I ask the boy. "What do you do when someone says you can't play?"

"Play alone. My mom told me to do that if people are mean."

"What if there was a rule that people can't act mean in that way—they have to let you play if you want to play? Would that be fair?"

Several children are waving their arms. "Yeah, it *is* fair," says one, "but some people don't like other people. So it would spoil the game."

"Once there was this boy in first grade," a girl recalls, "and he was making a newspaper and I asked him could I do it too and he said no to me and he told the two other kids yes. I felt bad."

"She could do it another time," a boy suggests, but his response irritates the girl.

"You always tell me that! How could I make a newspaper by myself? I couldn't even write good then. And *you* didn't let me come in your club yesterday anyways!"

"It wasn't me, it was Curtis." He points to a tall blond boy. "He's the boss. *He* says who comes in the club."

Curtis is uncomfortable. "I don't want to be the boss. *They* say I am."

"We call him the boss," the boy explains.

"Yeah, because I make up the game. They *wait* for me to make up the game. Then I have to pick everyone or say no."

"Does there have to be a boss?" I ask.

"Yeah, it's better," a girl responds. "Sometimes me and

Jamie play and we say there has to be a boss so if other people want to play and some people don't like that person whoever we pick to be the boss is the person to decide."

I find myself disturbed by this unchallenged acceptance of a boss. In the kindergarten, at least, the children argue or even cry about it. "Tell me," I say, "why exactly is a boss necessary?"

"If they didn't have bosses," a boy replies, "they could just vote." He contemplates the choices. "Or if it's someone everyone likes, they could just come in."

"If you are not a person everyone likes, then what gives you a better chance," I ask, "voting or a boss?" They all agree that voting usually works in favor of the person wanting to come in and is the fairest way to decide. But having a boss is much better.

My look of puzzlement brings on a sea of waving arms. One girl seems to speak for the group. "See, the bad thing about voting is, if you don't vote for that person she'll see all the people who don't like her. If it's a boss that's only *one* person doesn't like you so you don't feel so bad."

This is a novel thought: It is kinder to be rejected by only one classmate. Then you can still imagine that the others like you. "What if there were no bosses? And you didn't vote *or* choose. Whoever wanted to play could do so."

"That would be more fair," a boy agrees, "but it would be impossible to have any fun. It is a good rule though."

"Even if it spoils the fun?"

The girl who explained the reasonableness of having bosses has a quick answer. "It's a good rule because it's supposed to make people nicer."

I gaze at the sweet and innocent faces around the rug. These *are* nice children and, furthermore, they *do* know how the rejected ones feel. When I tell them about Clara, who sits in her cubby because she doesn't have a Pound Puppy and has been told she can't play, they are incensed.

"No fair!" a boy shouts. "They do that to my little sister and, boy, is my mom mad at the teacher for letting them."

"That's just an excuse about the dog," a girl says knowingly. "They just don't like her. It's like they're saying 'You're kind of *nasty!*'"

"Then should we have the rule in kindergarten?" I ask.

Everyone is in favor of this. "Sure, because those little kids will cry, like my sister."

"In second grade," a boy says, "you know how to handle yourself."

But a classmate is not sure. "What if you have a best friend that plays with you and then a new girl comes and then she starts playing with her all the time and they tell you no?"

Suddenly, we're back in the world of exposed feelings. "In kindergarten," says a small girl who has not spoken yet, "this girl Millie she didn't like me and she always said no to me when I asked her to play." The girl blushes and, for some reason, reminds me of Princess Annabella. If I were telling these children the Magpie stories would I make Annabella more vulnerable? Seven-year-olds seem to like the notion that children ought to be strong enough to handle bad feelings, yet they remember being rejected and worry about the least hurtful way of rejecting someone else. It does not occur to them that rejection itself is the problem.

"The second graders think we should definitely have a rule about letting everyone play," I tell the children the next day.

"Do they have the rule?" Charlie asks.

"No, they don't. In fact, they think it probably wouldn't work too well in second grade. They'd rather have a boss deciding who can play."

Even Lisa is surprised by the news. "They want a boss?"

"Yes, they say it's easier if one person decides who plays in a game. Then the child that the boss doesn't like won't think everyone doesn't like him, only the boss."

The children seem doubtful. They have accepted the fact that certain people call themselves bosses and are called bosses by others. But there is always some resistance, and the expectation that a boss will become too bossy after a while.

"They don't want *us* to have bosses, though," I add. "One boy said he didn't want anyone telling his little sister she couldn't play. And a girl remembered being sad in kindergarten when someone kept telling her she couldn't play with her."

"Let's not have bosses until we're in second grade," Waka says, looking at Charlie. But Charlie offers no response.

Annabella did not argue. She was an adventurous girl but also a sensible one. "Oh, Magpie," she said, as she lowered herself to the next ledge, "if only I could turn into a little moth as Beatrix does. Then I could fly with you to the eagle's nest."

Magpie hooted with delight. "Annabella, my girl, you've hit it! That's exactly what we've got: people as small as a moth. Uncle Orangerio can fly on my back up to the nest and hide while I perform my trick."

"What is the trick?" Annabella asked, but Magpie was already in the air.

"There's no time to explain," he shouted. "Just tell your father I'm about to put my special talent to the test!" Magpie flew quickly to the flower people and took Uncle Orangerio aside. He whispered and nodded and, finally, opened his wings to their fullest. Then Orangerio, to everyone's surprise, jumped on Magpie's back and in an instant the two were out of sight.

The moon slipped behind a cloud and soon the mountain itself disappeared in the dark. Suddenly out of the stillness came the shrill screeching of an eagle. "Kweek-kik-ik-ik-ik-ik! Kweek-kik-ik-ik-ik! Kweek, kweek!" Each time the call was heard it came from another place. The eagle seemed to be flying off in all directions. "Kweek-kik-ik-ik-ik-ik!" Then, with a swoosh of feathers, Magpie was back on the ledge, flattening his wings to allow Uncle Orangerio and the queen's son to dismount. "Open your eyes, little prince," Magpie said. "There is nothing to fear anymore."

Queen Orangelina hugged and kissed her child, crying and laughing all at once, until the boy bounced from her arms. "What an adventure!" he sang out, skipping around Magpie, pulling one person after another into his joyful dance.

The grateful queen shushed everyone for fear the eagle might hear them. "How did you do it, Magpie?" she asked.

Magpie shivered with excitement. "One of the things we magpies can do is imitate another bird's call. There are few birds we can't fool.

When the eagle heard what he imagined was another eagle intruding on his territory he was ready to fight. He flew angrily toward the sounds I was making but he got all mixed up because I kept changing my position, up and down, left and right."

"That's when I did my part," Uncle Orangerio stated proudly. "I crept into the nest and carried out the little prince, and then we hid inside a yellow flower until Magpie returned. I'll admit I was scared the whole time."

Magpie's eyes were shining. "The plan worked beautifully! Your talent and mine were a perfect match."

"My talent? What is my talent?" the tired little man wondered.

"Why, the talent of being so tiny!" Magpie exclaimed. "I could hardly feel your weight on my back. In fact, if you'll all hop aboard, I'll fly you down the mountain in a flash. Annabella's father will want to meet you before you return home. Let's be very quiet, shall we? We don't want to surprise an angry eagle in the dark."

They all looked up toward the eagle's nest from where an uncertain call could still be heard. "Kweek? Kweek? Kik-kik-ik-ik-ik?"

The third graders get to the point quickly. "Shirley is always rejected!" someone calls out and, before I realize what is about to occur, the group is awash in descriptions of the daily ordeals of an overweight, red-headed girl sitting directly to my left.

"In gym some girls scream and huddle under a blanket when she's coming in and they say 'She's coming! She's coming!'"

"They hide behind a tree and tease her. 'You can't even fit in here!'"

"They call her names."

"No one wants to eat lunch with her."

I motion for the children to stop. "Shirley, I'm sorry. Is this embarrassing you?"

Shirley surveys her classmates. "No, I want them to say it," she replies calmly. "They do reject me. No one wants me for a computer partner or to play jump rope—"

"But one time *she* brought this really long jump rope," a girl interrupts, "and lots of us wanted to play and we were standing watching and a couple of people she said they couldn't play."

"I said you have to wait!" Shirley exclaims. "There was too many."

"Shirley's not the only one. They reject me too!" A black boy is speaking. He is darker than Angelo but reminds me of him. "Me *and* her! We're both the ones they won't play with or anything."

"John bosses too much and he fights us!"

"Because you never want me to play!"

The discussion is as personal as those we have in kindergarten. The intense emotions surrounding the exclusion of Shirley and John are openly recognized; by fourth and fifth grade, the children will avoid direct confrontation. They'll refer to "the way people are" or even "the way girls are." One fourth grader will tell me "We're meaner than when we were young," without naming any victims.

Having exposed their worst offenses, the third graders settle down to examine variations on the theme of ordinary exclusion. "The other day, when the boys were playing baseball and I asked to play," a girl begins, "they said do you have a mitt and I said no and they said then I can't play."

"She could've got hurt," a boy replies.

"I could've borrowed a mitt."

"Then we wouldn't have even sides. Three and three."

"Couldn't you find another player?" I ask the girl. "To even the sides?"

"No one wanted to play," she answers.

"You didn't ask us," several girls protest.

"Because before that you said I couldn't play."

The baseball players want to set the record straight. "See, we just don't want odd teams."

"They don't want people they don't like," John complains. "They don't want me."

"They don't want girls. Except Jenny."

We all look at Jenny, who raises her hand but does not speak about baseball. "When I was in first grade this kid had candy and she was sharing it with me and then Holly came up and asked if she could have some and the girl said no and it hurt her feelings."

"Me? Was that me, Jenny?" Holly asks. "Oh, yeah, that *was* me."

"Your story is like the baseball incident," I tell Jenny.

"That's what made me think of it. People still aren't nice to Holly." The children look at Jenny warmly.

"Jenny is nice to Holly and to everyone," they inform me.

"Well, then, Jenny," I say, "do *you* think the plan would work? Could children learn to play with anyone who comes along without worrying about how much they like them?"

"Maybe," she answers slowly. "Only maybe. If they get to know each other better."

Her answer pleases John. "It *would* work if we could get along." His statement, heartfelt, almost pleading, is followed by silence.

Then Shirley adds, "If we could introduce each other better, I mean, *in advance.*"

"The rule *won't* work," a girl states. "If people don't like them and don't let them play, and if there's a rule, they'll tell the teacher and if the teacher makes them do it they just won't be nice to that person."

This reasoning will be restated often, especially in fourth and fifth grade. Forcing the issues of fairness or niceness is seen as counterproductive. But why, I wonder. A no-hitting rule doesn't produce more hitting. The children themselves enforce the rule. Even popular children can't get away with hitting.

"Okay," says a new speaker, "in a way it could work and in a way it wouldn't." She gropes for words a moment then expresses her idea quickly. "Some people—even me—want to own things. They say you can't come here and you can't come there. They say they are the boss and other people agree. Even me. If *that* stopped, then your plan could work."

"Not if you just don't *want* other people to play," a girl

argues. "They don't *like* them. Or, they just want to do something with two people. If the other person comes in, you won't be nice to them."

"See, your rule is very fair," a boy says, perhaps wanting me to feel good. "But some people don't get along and they just want to be with their friends. That's the most important thing to most people."

I turn to Shirley. "I've got to leave now but I'm going to let you have the last word, okay?" Shirley smiles at me and I realize how pretty she is.

"It might work and maybe not because some people would say, who cares about the rules, I'm playing with only my friend now." Then she looks at her teacher. "But it really might work because sometimes people are very nice to each other. Even to me."

The little prince could not keep his hands off of Maruska while the others drank tea and discussed every detail of the adventure over and over again. He petted her and climbed all over her. "Annabella, won't you come home with us, please?" he begged. "And won't you bring Maruska, too?"

"I'm sorry, Prince Orange Flower, but you see, we're on our way to a new home and we don't want to miss the boat."

When the little prince heard this, he sat down on the floor of the cave and began to cry. "I don't want them to go away!" he screamed in his tiny voice. Queen Orangelina was quite embarrassed. No matter what she said she could not comfort her son.

Then Magpie crouched low and murmured softly, "Would you like me to tell you a story? I will if you promise to stop crying." The tired little boy nodded and wiped his eyes. Magpie spoke to him in a voice that sounded like a lullaby.

Once there was a little boy who was brave and strong. When the three-horned lizard tried to enter his home the boy poked him with a sharp thorn sword and the lizard ran away. When a dragon blew fire in his face, the boy squirted him with a stinging liquid and the dragon cried and begged him to stop. One day the little boy saw a huge eagle steal a baby magpie from its mother and take it to a nest on the highest cliff. "I'll teach that monster a lesson," said the boy. He waited until the moon went behind a cloud and, faster than a mountain goat, he climbed to the eagle's nest. Then he roared a frightful roar and growled a terrible growl and the eagle flew away in alarm. "I've saved you, little magpie," the boy whispered. "You'll be back with your mother in a minute." And so he was. Then the boy went home to his own mother, who gave him a cup of hot nectar.

Prince Orange Flower laughed and hugged Magpie with his tiny arms. Then he took his mother's hand and she motioned to the others to follow them. "Thank you for your kindness," she said, bowing her head so low it seemed her crown would topple. "We must leave now. Our carriage is hidden under a bush just outside your cave."

Magpie was sorry to see the orange flower people leave. "I don't think that eagle will trouble you again," he said, flying above their miniature wagon, pulled by two fat toads. Annabella and the prince walked alongside until the turn in the road, then waved goodbye and returned to the cave. They were exhausted and fell asleep immediately.

The next day, at rug time, I tell the children about the third grade discussion. "They talked about two sad children in their class, a boy and a girl."

"Why are they sad?" Clara asks.

"Because no one wants to play with them. They don't want the boy on their baseball teams and they don't want the girl to be their computer partner or sit with them at lunch."

Angelo knows why. "They don't like those kids." The children look at me, waiting for more of an explanation.

"I think the third graders feel bad about not being kinder. That's why they talked about it so much. Anyway, these two children were not completely discouraged. The boy said, 'Your plan will work if we could all get along with each other.' And the girl said, 'Sometimes people are very nice to each other, even to me.'"

"What plan?" Jennifer asks.

"You can't say you can't play," I remind her. "It's not our plan yet. Or, rather, it's a plan but not a rule. We're *planning* for it. We're talking about it, getting opinions, thinking about it, wondering how it will work. I think that's a good way to start a new plan, if you've been doing something different all along."

Even as I speak I realize that these are rationalizations for my inability to move forward and proclaim the rule. Am I still worried that it is not fair? More likely, I worry that it won't work; I'll invite the children to celebrate my new rule and find that no one comes to the party.

My discussions with the older children have made me wary. How many more times will I be told, "Yeah, it's very fair, but I don't think it can work"? Friendship comes first, with fairness off somewhere in the distance. Yet in each class there seems to be a hopefulness, a light shining, a dream that they could reinvent Mrs. Wilson's backyard for themselves, a place where you are always asked, "Do you want to play?"

"Sarah, can the classroom be made to feel like your backyard?" I ask her.

"I think so but I'm not sure. At home the children come and go at will. Here we're stuck with each other all day."

"All the more reason, then. None of us can go home and we can't hide in our cubbies. We've got to depend on the kindness of strangers. Let's begin the new rule next week, when I've finished the discussions. I've got fourth grade tomorrow and fifth grade on Monday."

Waka tugs on my shirt. "I'm *not* following them!"

"He keeps following us," Ben complains.

"Waka just wants to play with you."

"We're playing *two* army bombers, me and Charlie."

I try a bit of humor. "Br-r-r! And here comes another one. Waka! The daring army bomber good guy!" The boys are laughing with me. I'm in such a good mood now they can't resist.

"Open your eyes, little prince," Magpie said. "There is nothing to fear anymore."

Early the next morning, Annabella helped her father repack the carriage and the three voyagers went quickly on their way. As they passed the sixth mountain, Annabella told the prince about the invisible seventh mountain. Magpie peered through the trees. "All I can see are some shadowy shapes in the distance," he said. "It certainly is odd, though. The sun is shining brightly everywhere else but not there. The orange flower people believe that there are lost dragons living there, Prince Kareem."

The prince turned to look at the dark cloud behind them. "It's possible, I suppose. If we can't see the mountain, perhaps whatever lives there cannot see the world outside. Unfortunately we have no time to investigate."

The travelers searched the horizon for the sea but even before they could see it they heard the distant sound of a ship's bell. "That must be the boat coming!" the prince shouted. "Magpie, would you fly ahead and ask them to wait for us? This is a piece of good luck."

The carriage arrived at the shore just as the ship was lowering its gangplank. A sailor marched the prince's horses up the wooden plank and then down into the ship's hold as Annabella and the prince joined the other passengers. The captain welcomed them. He seemed flustered and angry. "Is anything wrong?" the prince asked. "Can you take us across to the other side?"

"Of course," muttered the captain. He gave orders to his crew to

cast off the lines and move out. "That's my job. But it isn't my job to search for a thief, I can tell you!"

Annabella looked around as the boat began to sail; the people on the deck seemed quite ordinary. "A thief? What is the thief trying to steal?"

"Just some cheese and bread and tins of meat, but I don't like it!" The captain stamped his foot. "I run a tight ship, I do. If we've got an extra person on board, let him just come out and show himself. Or maybe it's not a stowaway after all!"

The captain glared suspiciously at the passengers, and Annabella whispered to her father, "He isn't very pleasant, is he? By the way, father, where is Magpie?"

"He's gone ahead to tell Alexandra and her parents that we're coming. He's certain the king and queen will have a place for us to live, perhaps even the thatched cottage he mentioned."

When she heard this, Annabella burst into song, an old sea chanty her mother had once taught her. "Four on a boat and the waves run high, look-a-way, look-a-way!"

The captain shushed her instantly. "Please, young lady! I'm in no mood for that. We've got a thief here and I mean to find him. Stay where you are, everyone. And please be quiet! My crew is about to begin a search. Quiet, I say!" The last warning was directed at Annabella.

In the fourth grade, the girls are certain that exclusion is primarily *their* problem. "The boys accept themselves much more," a girl says with conviction. "We're definitely meaner to each other. A girl is more likely to tell another girl she can't play." A group of girls giggle and nod their heads, causing me to wonder if they are teasing. It soon becomes clear, though, that they are serious.

A boy disagrees vehemently. Nothing in these discussions I've been having is ever said with indifference. "I don't think the girls do more rejecting. Say the boys are playing baseball and they don't want to let another boy in because he doesn't play so well, he's not good enough. Boys do that plenty of times." He doesn't say they do it to him but perhaps he would if he were still in third grade.

"Well, I watch the boys a lot," another girl says. "We're amazed, really. We even talk about it. The boys will hang around with any boy who comes up. Girls don't do that."

"It sounds to me," I say, "as if you wish you were more like that."

"I do. But, see, with girls there's always this feeling of having your own private little game just with your own friends. Some people feel that way. They don't want to play with everyone. They feel much better if they play with just a few good friends."

"What if someone doesn't have a few good friends?" I ask. "Wouldn't my rule give them some protection?"

"Oh, it's a good rule," a boy responds. "But it could spoil a game because someone might quit."

"It's a nice rule and it's fair but if there's a game and it's already overflowing with people—"

"—or there's not enough room—"

"The more people it's harder to manage. Every person has at least one problem. So the person who started the game might leave."

The girl who spoke up before the others flashes back: "So what! Aren't they leaving by choice? Look, I know I do it too! But the person who isn't allowed in doesn't even have a choice."

"Sure, Ruthie," says another girl, "but the first one is having a really good time and then it's all spoiled."

"That could happen," I admit, "but which is more important, that a person chooses to leave or that someone else isn't even allowed to enter?"

"Look, I do think it's right to have the rule," says a girl who appears troubled by what she is about to say. "But there are certain people who tend to have—there's something about certain people . . . I guess it frustrates . . . well, not to be insulting or anything but that person speaks in a way that's too—I mean, acts in a certain way . . . that spoils the game."

"Are you saying that the rule sounds right but, on the other hand, there are some people whose personal characteristics make them unpopular and you wouldn't want them to play?"

"But we do it to each other, even to our friends," a girl counters. "Sometimes you never know if someone is going to like you or not."

The boys have stopped talking. They are listening intently to the girls, their eyes moving from speaker to speaker. I point to one of the boys and ask, "Do you think rejection is more of a girl's problem?"

"No, I don't," he says. "Let's say I'm building a tower with

Harry and someone else comes along and wants to help us but we really want to play alone. But if they are really nice . . ."

"If who is nice?" I ask.

"Harry and me. If we are nice, we'd let him in. But what if that person doesn't play fair? Why should he be protected? I mean, even if he doesn't have friends he still has to act nice, doesn't he?"

Ruthie responds to his question. "I agree with you, but what if you can't act nice if you don't have friends? If my best friend rejects me because a new girl comes in, I feel pretty mean. Then I talk to my mom and dad about it and I feel better. What if certain people can't talk to their mom and dad?"

"That reminds me," says the girl next to Ruthie. "Remember when we were playing mean sisters and there was a really old sister and we pretended we locked her up and hid the key? We had four girls playing and someone came up and asked to play and we said no, for no reason! We said it was too late. But we could have added another role."

"You just wanted best friends?" I ask. "Or is there a habit of saying no, perhaps? By the way, I see you're still playing the sort of pretend games we play in kindergarten. That was a Cinderella theme, wasn't it? Some girls in my class play Cinderella all the time but everyone wants to be Cinderella and not the mean sisters."

The children laugh and Ruthie says, "We get more practice being mean."

"You sound serious," I tell her.

"I am. We're much meaner than in kindergarten."

I consider her statement for a while. "Then why am I so sure we need the rule?"

"I don't mean they act that nice to *each other*. But they're nice enough to follow a new rule. They trust you. They'll do what you say. It's too late to give *us* a new rule."

"She's right," a boy says. "If you want a rule like that to work, start at a very early age. Even nursery school. My little sister could do it."

There are nods of agreement around the rug. "Yeah, start it in kindergarten," someone says. "Because they'll believe you that it's a *rule*. You know, a *law*."

The prince approached the blustery boatman. "Excuse me, sir," he said politely. "Will it be necessary to search us? We've only just come aboard."

The captain grunted. "I suppose not. You'll be disembarking in a few minutes anyway." Then he called to the crew to hold up the search until the newcomers got off. The boat arrived at the shore and a sailor led the prince's horses out of the hold and across the gangplank to the dock. Magpie was there to greet them, flying back and forth in front of a row of tall pines. Below him stood a girl with hair the color of the yellow flowers that grew in the cracks of the rocks Annabella had climbed. Now, thought Annabella, the next part of our adventure begins: a real school, a new friend . . . what else will happen? Her thoughts were interrupted by the horses, who suddenly reared up and whinnied.

"They may have heard some splashing under the dock," the prince said. "Perhaps they saw an alligator or something like that."

However, when Annabella reached into the carriage for Maruska's shawl, she discovered the blankets were all tangled up and splattered with mud. "Father, someone has been in our carriage. Do you think it was that thief the captain was looking for?"

The prince looked under the dock and along the beach but he could see nothing. "Well, we've no time for this mystery, child. Here comes Magpie and a young lady who must be the princess. Magpie! Alexandra! You can't imagine how happy we are to be here at last!"

The girls reached out and clasped hands tightly. "Welcome to the Kingdom of Tall Pines," said Alexandra. "My mother and father are preparing rooms for you at the castle."

Annabella thanked her and glanced about. "Where is Beatrix?" she asked. "When will we meet her?"

Magpie seemed embarrassed. "Uh . . . she's not quite ready to greet you," he replied, and Alexandra burst out laughing.

"Beatrix is never ready to greet anyone new in her dear Magpie's life. When she first met me, she tried to turn me into a frog, but luckily that was too hard for her."

Annabella looked anxiously at Magpie, who quickly reassured her. "Nothing to worry about, Annabella. Beatrix won't bother you at all. She just needs a bit of time to get used to people."

Hidden nearby behind a tree sat a very jealous Beatrix, glowering at the newcomers. "Don't be too sure of me, Magpie," she muttered. "I'm not nearly as nice as you think I am."

Lisa dictates a mousie story. "Once upon a time there were five mousie sisters and five mousie brothers. Two of their sisters were babies and two of the brothers were babies. They were newborns. The older sisters and brothers brought them blueberries and tucked them into bed and read them stories at bedtime. One day a kitty that had no mother or father and was an orphan asked if she could be a sister and they said yes. The end."

I gaze at Lisa in admiration. "In your stories you let everyone play."

She smiles and begins to draw pictures of tiny mice in the margins of the page. "Beatrix is jealous, you know," Lisa says, suddenly, as if we have been discussing Magpie's witch friend all along. "That's the reason she thinks she's not nice. Jealous people don't feel nice."

"That's interesting," I comment. "I wonder what makes a person jealous."

"You know, if you can't have someone all to yourself. When I'm jealous I'm not nice."

"Beatrix does do nice things," I remind her. "She took care of Magpie just like the big brothers and sisters in your story take care of the newborns. Are those teensy mice the newborns, Lisa?" She has drawn exactly ten mice and one small cat, the characters in her story. "Lisa, this gives me an idea. Wait here a moment." I go to my book bag and take out a large sketchbook into which I've been copying the Magpie stories, with the idea of asking Sarah to do some illustrations. She is a fine artist, besides being a fine teacher. But I think it might be even nicer to ask the children to draw pictures in the margins as Lisa is doing.

There are now half a dozen or more children at the story table. Young children are profoundly attuned to any new behavior on the part of the adults who care for them. My determined trip to the book bag and the large unfamiliar book under my arm are all it takes to bring a parade of children to my side.

I turn the pages slowly. "Look, these are the Magpie stories. I'm copying them, one chapter at a time, into this drawing pad so that there will be room for illustrations—pictures that I hope you'll draw for the book. Little pictures, because the words take up most of the space." I continue to turn the pages until I come to today's chapter. "Here, this says, 'The king and queen offered Prince Kareem and Annabella an unused part of the castle for their new home but the prince asked instead for the thatched cottage that stood empty at the edge of the forest.' This is the way the chapter begins. Now, see all the space on all these pages for drawings?"

"I want to draw the orange flower people," Angelo says. "And the eagle too. Can we make as many as we want?"

"Absolutely. I can use them all. Just draw them small enough to fit in these margins, cut them out and give them to me. I'll find the words they belong to and tape them nearby."

Lisa has a picture of Magpie for me even before I finish speaking. "This is fine," I tell her. "It may be a bit large but we can put it here, in the top corner." I measure Magpie from beak to tail with a ruler. "How many inches is Lisa's picture of Magpie?" I ask, and everyone seems to know it is three inches. "Okay, now the margins are three inches—look here, do you see?—on the right side of the page and two inches on the left. After you draw a picture, measure it and see which side of the page it goes on. If your picture is even larger, don't worry, because I'm leaving a big space at the end of each chapter."

There is a sudden rush for paper, crayons, markers, and scissors and then the room is filled with the quiet monologues of busy artists. "This is Annabella, she's got a pink ribbon in her hair and a blue dress on. Now here comes the orange flowers . . ." "K-k-k, watch out, the eagle! K-k-k." Ah, yes. If the room were always like this there would be no need for our new rule. Everyone is occupied with individual projects directed toward a goal created by the teacher. No one is excluded; every contribution will be given equal attention and find equal expression in the margins of the Magpie story. No problems here. The rule is needed for all those other times, the bulk of the day, when public and private needs and obligations are in conflict.

Lisa is drawing her third picture of Beatrix. She can't get it quite the way she wants it but she's not at all impatient, as she tends to be with people. "By the way, Lisa, I just remembered something really nice you did for Hiroko. When she hurt her knee you sat with her and looked at a book with her. That made her feel much better. You were her friend for a long time on that day."

"Who's nicer, me or Beatrix?"

"You both do nice things."

"Is she going to hurt Annabella?" Lisa looks worried. Would she tell Annabella she can't play, preferring Alexandra? My thought is not a nice one, but Lisa does seem to prefer blond girls. She never chooses Jennifer, who is black, to be in her stories, nor will she pick Angelo to be a father or brother. But she doesn't pick Clara or Nelson either and they are both pale blonds. What all these children may have in common, as far as Lisa is concerned, is that they are outsiders, different in some way from the children she has known. No, this is not true. They are *not* different. What makes them outsiders is simply that they are *treated* as outsiders.

"I can see you're a bit anxious about Beatrix and Annabella," I say. "She almost does something bad . . ."

Lisa jumps up, laughing. "Oh, no! Magpie won't ever let her be mean to Annabella. I just know that!" And she runs off to play.

Who is this Magpie who won't let Beatrix be mean? Someone apparently who is more powerful than jealousy and more dependable than impulse and caprice. Lisa likes Magpie and trusts him. His is the first picture she draws for the book. I am certain she wants me to be more like Magpie and not allow her to be mean even when she is jealous of playmates or uncomfortable with strangers.

The king and queen offered Prince Kareem and Annabella an unused part of the castle for their new home but the prince asked instead for the thatched cottage that stood empty at the edge of the forest. "I wish to live as close to the birds as I can," he explained.

Every day after school, Alexandra walked home with Annabella. The prince would be waiting for them near the bird feeder, drawing pictures of the hungry, noisy birds. When he saw the girls he always said, "Well, I've fed the birds and now it's time to feed the humans. Tea is ready, children. Big cups or little?" Annabella still preferred her tea in Maruska's doll cups.

One day, as they strolled along, hand in hand, Alexandra said, "I wish we were sisters."

Annabella smiled and replied, "It's even nicer to be friends. But we can pretend to be sisters. Let's pretend we're walking in the forest and—"

"And pretend we have no mother or father," Alexandra continued, "and then we find a baby bear who is lost and we take him home. Maruska can be the bear."

Annabella bent down to take up a handful of moss. "And we pick blueberries for supper," she said. She had never actually picked blueberries, but when she played with Alexandra it often seemed the nicest thing they could pretend to do. "Pretend this is the blueberries," she told her friend, giving her the moss.

Beatrix heard the girls from behind her tree and she was jealous. "I hate those girls," she told Magpie.

He was troubled. "But, Beatrix, they've done nothing bad to you."

"Yes, they have," she snapped angrily. "They love each other and pretend things together and I have no friend but you, Magpie, which isn't the same. Those girls make me mad. I just know I'm going to do something mean."

Magpie flew around Beatrix's face. "Tell me what," he urged, but the young witch shook her head.

"Never mind, I haven't decided," she replied. "Go away now. I want to be alone."

Yet Beatrix had already begun her mischief. As soon as Magpie was gone, she uncovered the hole she'd been digging next to the path the girls took through the forest. The hole would soon reach her underground tunnel. "Now, what would make Annabella leave the path?" Beatrix asked herself as she dug. One more jab with the shovel and she suddenly knew: a blueberry bush! Annabella was always pretending to pick blueberries.

Beatrix had enough magic to make a blueberry bush appear but not as much magic as she might have had if she'd studied harder in witch's school. "You'll never be a truly fine witch," her mother would warn, "if you don't pay attention."

"I'm too lonely," was Beatrix's reply. "No one likes me." And the old witch mother would shake her head. "But, child, witches aren't supposed to be liked. Your sisters don't care if they're liked. This simply isn't our way."

Now, as she piled more branches over the hole, Beatrix was sorry her mother wasn't there to see the trick she was about to play on the princesses. She blinked three times and a bush filled with ripe blueberries appeared. That was easy, she thought. The problem was how to make only Annabella fall into the trap.

As it happened, however, both girls tumbled into the hole. Actually, one fell and the other jumped. Annabella spied the blueberries first. "Oh, look! I didn't know there were—oh, help, I'm falling!"

Alexandra watched with horror as her friend disappeared through the branches. "Wait for me!" she called. "I'm coming too!" The girls dropped onto a pile of leaves and got up quickly. "This trap must have been meant for an animal," Alexandra said.

"No!" screamed Beatrix, leaping out in front of them. "I made it for Annabella. And you spoiled everything, you naughty Alexandra. I don't know why Magpie likes you!"

Alexandra was outraged. "You're the naughty one, Beatrix! You set a trap and caught us."

Beatrix wailed and stamped her feet. "No, no! I just wanted Annabella. Oh, I should have studied harder in witch's school."

Annabella examined the tall, strange-looking girl with great interest. "You needn't feel bad then, Beatrix," she said, "because I'm the only one who did fall into your trap. Alexandra jumped."

Beatrix was astonished. "Jumped? Why did you jump, Alexandra?"

"So I could help Annabella," she replied, and Beatrix's face reddened.

"There, you see?" she cried. "No one ever does things like that for me. I don't have a single friend. Except Magpie, but he doesn't exactly count. I thought if you fell in, Annabella, and had no one else to play with, you might be lonely and become my friend. But you spoiled everything, Alexandra." And Beatrix began to cry.

Alexandra was surprised to see that witches cry just the way ordinary children do. "I'm truly sorry, Beatrix. You must have worked very hard to dig that big hole and make a blueberry bush appear." She brushed some cobwebs from the young witch's dress and smoothed her messy hair. "You really are a clever witch after all."

Then Annabella took Beatrix's hand. "Would you like to come to the cottage for tea tomorrow? Father is going to try my mother's recipe for sugar cookies."

Beatrix's eyes widened in astonishment. "Are you inviting me to tea? A tea party?" She began to turn cartwheels down the long tunnel.

"Wait for us, Beatrix!" the girls shouted. "Where are you going?"

"Follow me!" she called. "This is the way out." When the girls climbed through the opening, they found Beatrix telling Magpie about the tea party. "Do you think they'll want me to be their friend?" she whispered anxiously.

Magpie turned to Annabella. "How will your father feel about Beatrix coming to tea after he hears about the trap she set? Are you sure he'll want her?"

Annabella skipped out in front. "Why, Magpie, father is just like you. When he finds out that Beatrix is lonely, he'll probably invite her to tea every day."

"Why, Magpie, father is just like you. When he finds out that Beatrix is lonely, he'll probably invite her to tea every day."

On my early morning run, the rhyme jogs along in rhythm with my feet on the pavement: You can't say you can't play, you can't say you can't play. Am I ready to stand alongside Magpie and Prince Kareem, defending the rights of the lonely to come to the tea party? To be barely tolerated by a teacher would be bad enough; to be rejected by one's classmates is the saddest tale of all.

But can this kind of morality be legislated? And what about that other moral imperative: the right to choose one's companions, unpressured and unopposed? Well, you can still choose your own companions. No one is telling you *not* to play with someone.

And yet, is there not a natural desire to include certain people and exclude others? Or is this desire in the same category as, say, biting? Some two-year-olds have a strong need to bite people; when they learn to curb the impulse they are much relieved. Perhaps being destructive is a burden. Yes, it must surely come as a relief when one's good times are no longer predicated upon someone else's bad times. That is, *if* the comparison to biting is correct.

So much of teaching straddles the moral fence: Should I or shouldn't I? Is it right or wrong, fair or unfair, proper or improper? No more, on this issue at least. I stand fast—run fast?—on this decision. It shall be added to my headstone. "Here lies a schoolteacher in whose time 'You can't say you can't play' was put into rhyme."

The image makes me laugh out loud; I'm surely on a runner's high. Never mind, *this* will be the day I'll impose the rule, after Sarah reads the new Magpie chapter. It is about Raymond, the boy nobody likes. *"Our class was much nicer before he came."*

I wonder how Lisa will feel about Raymond. Yesterday she told me, "But some children aren't nice enough to play with. They're too—uh, rough, I mean, too sad."

"Maybe being sad makes you feel not nice to play with," I suggest. "A fourth grade girl said that's the way she is."

"But when I have to be with sad children then it makes me sad," Lisa explains. "And when I know I'm going to be sad then I'm always more sadder."

Lisa has identified the feeling. And the sadder people become the more we'd like not to be around them. So, then, if we set out specifically and openly to make children *less* sad by giving them the keys to the kingdom . . . well, we shall see.

The next day at tea the girls could speak of nothing else but the new red-haired boy. "I wish you could make him disappear, Beatrix," Alexandra said. "Our class was much nicer before he came."

Beatrix had never been to the little schoolhouse the girls attended. In her own witch's school bad behavior was taught along with reading and writing, but she realized that in the world outside, good behavior was preferred. "What sort of things does he do?" she asked, taking her third sugar cookie from the platter the prince was passing around.

"Well," Alexandra replied, in a huff, "he tore my picture and he broke Annabella's chalk and he knocked over her chair and he pushes the boys and . . . oh, why did he have to come?"

The new boy's name was Raymond. No one knew where he came from or where he lived, and all the children were complaining about him. There was only one school in the Kingdom of Tall Pines, with a single classroom and teacher called Schoolmistress. Fifteen children since Annabella had arrived—and now, with Raymond, sixteen—of all ages did their lessons and played together in one large room. The Olders helped the Youngers learn to read and write and the Youngers helped the Olders with the chores, which included feeding the chickens that Schoolmistress kept in the schoolyard, chopping wood, and weeding the garden. "I'm not a Younger, and I'm not an Older!" Raymond had protested on his first day, refusing to help with the chores. Schoolmistress raised her eyebrows but said nothing.

"That boy should be punished!" Alexandra told Magpie, and Beatrix liked the idea.

"Why don't you knock over his chair?" she suggested. "And give him a push. I'd teach him a thing or two!"

"That's nonsense, Beatrix," Magpie argued. "You'd only be teaching him what he already knows."

Beatrix did not agree. "That boy needs some of my nasty tricks. Shall I show you a few, girls? You'll make him sorry he ever came to your school, I promise you that."

The prince had been listening with much interest. "Shall we invite this new boy to tea, Annabella? I'll show him my bird books and he can come bird watching with me. That should put him in a better mood."

After school the next day, Annabella stopped Raymond on the steps and invited him to tea. Raymond looked surprised, but then he frowned. "Why does your father want me to come? Didn't you tell him how bad everyone thinks I am?"

Annabella nodded. "I did, but he still wants you. He thinks you might also like to go on a bird walk."

"Well, I don't!" Raymond kicked the dirt angrily. "And I don't *want any tea!" He stormed through the flower bed and kept running until he was deep in the forest.*

Then Raymond threw himself on the ground and began to cry. A voice came from the branches above. "Can you help me, young man? My name is Magpie." Raymond wiped his eyes and stared at Magpie. "A baby raccoon is trapped in a cage and I need someone with hands to release the spring on the lock. Will you come?"

Raymond got up and followed Magpie to the whimpering little animal. "You'll have to work fast. I hear footsteps not too far away."

The boy struggled with the rusty lock. "One more twist and I'll have it open," he said. The baby raccoon came up to Raymond and licked his fingers. "There! Come out, little one, and run quickly to your mother." Then Raymond sighed to himself, "You're lucky to have your mother with you."

Magpie pretended not to have heard him. Instead he said, "Thank you, Raymond. You are *the new boy, aren't you? That was a good job you did."*

"Yeah, well, I have to go," Raymond muttered.

Magpie could tell he was embarrassed. What an unusual boy, he thought. "Is your mother waiting for you?" he asked, but Raymond walked away.

Then, without turning around, he called out, "Sure, she's waiting for me."

After a few moments, Magpie quietly followed Raymond to a dense area of tangled roots and hanging moss. The boy looked all around him, then pushed aside some large branches that covered the entrance to a small cave and went inside. Magpie watched as Raymond arranged his schoolbooks on a splintered crate. Then the boy took an apple from a pile collected on a flat rock and lay down on a bed of moss and pine needles.

It was clear to Magpie that no mother lived in this cave. It was also clear that Raymond was the ship's thief Annabella had told him about. There were six tins of meat stacked up next to the apples and the name of the ship was still on them.

But Raymond was not thinking about that scary time on the boat. He stared up at the ceiling of the cave and thought about the baby raccoon. "I liked helping that little animal," he said aloud. "Tomorrow in school I'm going to help someone." Then he smiled for the first time since he had hidden himself on the boat, and fell into a deep sleep.

The New Order Begins

The fifth grade discussion has had to be postponed for a week, so I'm glad I decided not to wait. The children stare at the sign on the wall above the piano as I point to each word. "YOU CAN'T SAY YOU CAN'T PLAY. There. Our new rule. In big letters. We've been talking about it and now it's time to do it."

The children are uneasy, looking at one another. The announcement seems too abrupt, though we've been preparing ourselves for weeks. "Here's an example of what the rule means," I say. "Remember when Lisa and Cynthia told Clara she couldn't play because she didn't have a puppy? And—"

"And Ben wouldn't let me be in the dinosaur club," Angelo calls out.

"And Smita said I couldn't sit next to her," Clara recalls.

"Well, Sheila wouldn't be my partner either that time," Smita answers, in justification.

The children do not need examples from me. I smile encouragingly. "Now we'll know what to do when these things happen. You see, the rule probably won't keep them from going on, but it will tell us what is the fair thing to do when they happen."

"It's not fair at all." Lisa pouts. "I thought we were only just *talking* about it. I just want my own friends. What if someone isn't nice and hits me?"

"Lisa, we understand how you feel. But you'll always be able to play with the children you like best. Nothing changes about that. And we already have a rule about hitting. You remember what that is, don't you?"

Charlie speaks up. "If you hit once it could be a mistake or an accident. But if you hit again you have to leave the game."

Lisa is not impressed. "There's some people I don't like."

"You don't like me," Angelo says without emotion, and everyone looks at him as if acknowledging the sad truth of his statement. Very well, let this be the test: When Lisa accepts Angelo into her play or story, it will be a sign that the rule is working. Meanwhile I'll demonstrate my belief that the rule is fair for everyone equally.

"You know, I have to change something *I've* been doing," I tell the children, so softly they move closer as if on a rolling platform. They have grown accustomed to my new, quieter voice. "I have to make a big change myself. Something I'm doing doesn't fit the new rule." My confession startles them. A bit of the unexpected works wonders when Act I of a new drama begins.

"You have all watched how upset I become with Karl when he won't clean up the blocks."

"Then he can't play there until he does," Sheila says.

"Right." I point to the sign. "However, if you can't say you can't play, then even I mustn't tell Karl not to play."

"But what if he doesn't clean up?" Clara asks.

"Well, what should happen?"

Charlie is first to reply. "Nothing."

"Nothing at all?"

"Nothing," he repeats. "Let him read a book."

I stare at Charlie in surprise. "You're being kind to Karl but before you wouldn't let him be a Ninja Turtle."

"I said he could tomorrow."

"No you didn't," Karl says. "I was listening."

"Anyway, the new rule isn't nice," Lisa persists.

"You'd like to be able to tell people they can't play," I state simply.

"No, I don't," she argues. "Only to say it nicely so they don't feel bad. In a nice voice."

"And shall I tell Karl in a nice voice that he can't play if he doesn't clean up?"

Lisa shakes her head. "Cleaning up isn't the same thing."

"Of course not, Lisa. It isn't a good enough reason to keep a kindergarten child from playing. He will eventually learn to clean up. Maybe even tomorrow." I smile at Karl. "But, Lisa, I also agree with Angelo. He said when you're not allowed to play you feel lonely and you get water in your eyes. And if you're lonely and sad I'm afraid you can't learn very much or behave very well."

"Like Raymond the new boy," Lisa says. "He only has Magpie to be his friend."

"You forgot the baby raccoon," adds Angelo. "Hey, that fox! I want it to be a baby raccoon!" He jumps up and gets his notebook, bringing me a pencil so I can immediately make the change in his hunter story.

Whenever a child refers to the Magpie stories, I feel enormously grateful. This must be the way the children feel when we talk about their stories. My voice is sufficiently improved now that I can read to the children, and the process seems more complete. Writing the stories is not enough for me, nor is listening to Sarah read them. I need a direct connection, the sort the children create when their stories are acted out—and, even more so, when they know they will be allowed to play and to take the role they wish.

All along the path to school, Raymond imagined himself doing helpful things and the children smiling back at him in surprise. Just wait, he thought, you'll see how nice I can be.

A girl sat on the school steps struggling with the tiny buttons on a doll's dress. "Here, I'll do that," he offered, but when he took the doll from her, a button popped off. "Oh, I'm sorry, I didn't mean to . . ."

"Can't you ever be nice, Raymond?" she demanded, scowling at him. He moved indoors quickly.

At the carpentry bench a boy was gluing the parts of a boat together and Raymond could see he was making a mistake. "You're putting the rudder on backwards," he pointed out. "I can help you with that."

"Leave it alone, Raymond, don't touch it!" the boy warned, but Raymond reached for the glue.

"Let me show you how. My father used to . . ."

"Don't show me!" the boy screamed, pulling his boat away with

one hand and pushing Raymond with the other. As he did, the pieces split apart. "See what you made me do!"

Raymond looked around frantically, then burst out crying. "Nobody lets me be nice!" he sobbed, rushing from the room. He ran and ran until he reached the woods. "Magpie, Magpie, I need you!" he shouted.

Beatrix looked up from her game of tiddly-winks she'd made out of little stones. "Why are you calling Magpie?" she asked.

Raymond was startled to see a messy-haired girl seated next to the path. "I have to talk to him," he told her. "I'm Raymond."

Beatrix hid her game under a bush. "Ah, the naughty boy. The girls told me all about you. I can be pretty bad myself so I know a lot about these things."

"They all yell at me," he explained, "even if it's an accident."

Beatrix pulled on Raymond's shirt and made him sit down next to her on the ground. "Well, there's the problem, my boy. Now, listen to me. Always do your mischief on purpose because no one believes you if you say it's an accident."

At that moment, Magpie flew by and landed on a rock next to Raymond. The boy quickly told him everything. "Hmm, I see," said Magpie, nodding his head. "What a day you've had. Too bad, too bad."

"Now everyone thinks I'm a crybaby," the boy said.

Magpie shook his head even more vigorously. "You needn't worry about that. Annabella and Alexandra make each other cry several times a week. And then they're friends again."

"You don't understand, Magpie," Raymond argued. "I have no friends to begin with, so how can I become friends again?"

"I want to be Lisa's friend and she won't let me," Hiroko says the moment I stop reading.

Lisa defends herself. "We needed only a certain number of ponies."

"She promised me and then she forgot."

"These kids," Angelo says disapprovingly. "They'll always forget sometimes when they tell you. My daddy he say just don't play if they doesn't want you."

"Angelo, tell your daddy about the new rule. He'll really like it, I know. Because he wants this school to be fair to everyone."

"Does Schoolmistress have the rule?" Lisa asks.

"No, she doesn't."

"Why not?"

"Maybe she hasn't thought enough about it. By the way, I think the new rule will get us out of a trap like the one Beatrix made. She wanted to capture Annabella and keep Alexandra out. Well, if you try to keep someone out of your game then it's like a trap that keeps you and your friends *in*. Beatrix was so sure she'd be happy if only she could have Annabella all to herself, but it turned out she was much happier when both girls *and* Prince Kareem became her friends. And soon she'll have Raymond for a friend also."

It is clear to me that I am avoiding Lisa's question. Why doesn't Schoolmistress have the rule? Shall I write a chapter in which the teacher posts a rule as I have done and

Raymond's classmates stop excluding him? How can I have Schoolmistress's children so easily persuaded when mine may not be? Better to let the children play along the edges of our new rule for a while. Its complexities are great; I must not trifle with the subject.

My discussion with first through fourth grades has convinced me of two certainties: The rule is essential and it must begin at this intuitive stage of learning, when, as the fourth grade girl said, "They're nice enough to follow a new rule. They trust you." If I'm so certain, why not let Schoolmistress try it out? The answer is obvious. I can't have her succeed and me fail.

"I'm your friend, Raymond," Magpie said. "How about you, Beatrix?"

The witch jumped up and grabbed Raymond's hand. "Sure I am. You want to play pretend with me like the girls do?"

Magpie was pleased with Beatrix's idea. "Do you like to pretend things, Raymond?"

The boy did not answer for a moment. Then he said, "There is one thing I pretend all the time, Magpie, that I'm a lost baby dragon looking for its father."

Beatrix clapped her hands. "Is there a bad dragon in this pretend game? That's what I want to be."

"Yes, there is, and Magpie, you can be the father. I have to find you before the bad dragon comes to steal the magic." Raymond looked up and saw Annabella and Alexandra running up the path.

"What's going on here?" they called. "Schoolmistress told us to look for you, Raymond."

Beatrix was already on her hands and knees, growling. "We're playing with Raymond," she said proudly. "He's the baby dragon who's lost and Magpie is the father but the baby dragon didn't find him yet and I'm the bad dragon."

The girls were eager to play, too. "Can we be sisters, Raymond? Dragon sisters?"

Raymond hesitated a moment as if wondering whether or not he could trust Annabella and Alexandra to be in his game. But when he saw that they were Magpie's friends, he said, "Sure, just get down like this and you have to make a noise like this when you're angry. Kushshsh! Like a fiery snort." Soon the young princesses were on all fours, roaring at unseen enemies, and following all of Raymond's movements.

None of the players noticed the arrival of Prince Kareem until he plopped down beside them with his basket. "Ah, you found the young man," he said breathlessly. "Schoolmistress said everyone was mean to you today, Raymond, but you seem happy enough now. I've brought some tea things. Let me spread this cloth out on a flat rock. Magpie, I hope you have a story for us today."

Raymond was surprised to hear that Magpie was a storyteller. "What kind of stories do you tell?" he asked. "Are they true stories, about real things?"

Magpie fluffed his feathers and looked at Raymond. "You can decide for yourself. I think I'll tell one today about a baby dragon."

Raymond was unable to mask his pleasure. "Did you get the idea from me?" he asked.

"Yes, I did. Let me sip a bit more tea while my thoughts connect to one another." After a few moments Magpie began.

There was once in the land of six mountains a baby dragon whose father wanted him to be a fierce fighter. Every day the father told him stories of great battles and showed him how to breathe fire. On the little dragon's fourth birthday the father said, "My son, you are now old enough to go to war. We must fight the blue-humped dragons, for they are taking water from our mountain. Their own streams and rivers are drying up."

The little dragon laughed. "Let them have the water, father. We have more than we need."

Never had the father heard such talk; he decided to take his son into battle immediately. However, when they came within sight of the enemy, the boy refused to breathe fire and smoke. "I order you to breathe fire!" the father shouted, and the little dragon tried to obey him. He took a deep breath and exhaled as forcefully as he could, but instead of fire a wisp of pink smoke emerged and carried him up to the sky. "Come down, come down," the father cried, but a dark cloud covered the mountain and the sky could no longer be seen.

The father knelt down and wept for his lost child, and soon a small blue-humped dragon came and sat beside him. "May I drink from your stream?" he asked.

"Yes, yes," the father replied. "Of what good are my possessions if my child is gone?" The blue-humped dragon took one sip and instantly the cloud lifted. A rainbow dipped down and touched the mountain, bringing the warrior's son back to him.

Is this a dream? the father wondered, but he knew he must change *his ways. "Come! You may drink from our streams," he called to his surprised neighbors. "My son would like us to be friends."*

When the story was over, Raymond got up and began to walk away. "Where are you going?" Annabella asked. "Don't you want to play dragon again?"

"I have to leave," the boy mumbled. "My uncle is waiting for me." Then he disappeared quickly into the forest.

It Is Easier to
Open the Door

Sarah and I can't believe that the transition to the new rule is so straightforward and easy. "You can't say you can't play" has been in place for a week and there are only minor mishaps, quickly resolved. It is indeed a ladder out of the trap we've been in. Exclusion is still practiced, of course, but when it is someone will say "You forgot the rule," or a teacher will be brought over to say it. What joy to be rid of the burden of indecision.

I remember feeling this way some ten years ago, when I gave up the time-out chair, my version of "You can't play." Sarah jokes that I substituted six little words for endless arguing simply in order to save my voice, but I do think the image of escape from a trap is appropriate. When the children are reminded of the rule they comply so readily that it is as if they've been rescued. From what? Perhaps from the ordeal of deciding whether or not someone can play, just as doing away with the time-out chair relieved me of the onus of judging punishable actions.

Lisa continues to be a barometer, reminding children of the rule under certain circumstances and crusading for the old order at other times. She worries about losing ground if she

gives up control and she is more aware of the ordinary inse-
curities others feel.

"Now Cynthia likes Mary Louise better than me," she complains as we walk to the gym.

"They didn't want you to play?"

"Not that, but Cynthia plays with Mary Louise whenever
I'm doing something by myself. And I feel like that she's a
teensy bit better friend now to Cynthia."

"I'm sure Cynthia is still a good friend to you, Lisa."

"But I didn't realize she likes Mary Louise so much." Lisa
shrugs her shoulders. "I didn't used to know this before."

"You'd rather have Cynthia all to yourself," I say gently.

"I just want her to like me more than Mary Louise."

"Did you ask to play?"

"They were coloring and I didn't want to. But then, anyway,
Clara came and first they said no, then Mrs. Wilson told them
the rule."

"I bet that made you feel better."

"Sort of. But I still wish we didn't have the rule." I put my
arm around Lisa. "Look, I know you don't feel the way Clara
does. She's much happier, I think. She was hardly in her
cubby this week. And Angelo told me he likes the new rule
and so does his father."

Lisa raises her eyebrows. "Could I give an opinion?" she
asks in her most polite voice. "We could change the rule, not
too much change it, but kind of like change it this way. We
could say yes you could play if you really really really want
to play so much that you just take the part the person in
charge wants you to be." She takes for granted there must be

a child "in charge." How long will it take to get rid of the notion of a boss? The fourth grade girl who labeled herself as an "owner" said this is where the problem lies. Do away with owners and the rule could work, she told everyone.

Lisa skips ahead and then returns to take my hand. "I know Magpie likes the new rule, right? He'll tell Schoolmistress about it, because he's nice." *I* like the rule too, though I'm not nearly as nice as Magpie. However, each time a cause for sadness is removed for even one child, the classroom seems nicer. And, by association, we all rise in stature. Why not assume the children feel as I do? When I was in that first grade classroom fifty-five years ago it would have been an enormous relief to me if the fat girl with only one dress had been treated kindly.

Thinking about unkindness always reminds me of the time-out chair. It made children sad and lonely to be removed from the group, which in turn made me feel inadequate and mean and—I became convinced—made everyone feel tentative and unsafe. These emotions show up in a variety of unwholesome ways depending on whether one is a teacher or child. We are all cut from the same cloth. The time-out chair was my means of punishment. "You can't play" is the child's way. If it is wrong for me to exclude, then it is equally wrong for the children. Another classroom trap has been eliminated.

The next day after school, the girls ran along the forest path looking for Magpie. "Where are you, Magpie?" they called, stopping at the

flat rock he and Beatrix often used as a meeting place. "Magpie! Beatrix! Isn't anyone here?"

"What's all the excitement?" Beatrix asked from behind a tree.

The girls were relieved to see her. "Oh, good, it's you, Beatrix. We've come to find Raymond. He wasn't in school today and we think Magpie knows where he lives."

"He does indeed," Beatrix replied. "But you won't find either of them here right now. They're with your father, Annabella. Come on, I'll go with you."

When Beatrix and the girls arrived at the cottage the prince and Magpie were deep in conversation with Raymond. "So, you see, Prince Kareem is absolutely correct," Magpie was saying. "There's no question about it."

"Yes, dear boy," the prince added, "you must listen to reason. Why, you only need to think of your mother. How would she feel if she knew you lived in a cave?"

"Do you and your uncle live in a cave?" Annabella asked Raymond.

"I lied about my uncle," he said. "I did live with him before I came here, but I ran away."

The girls gasped in surprise. "Ran away? Why?"

"Because he didn't want me to keep searching for my father. Everyone says my father died in battle, but my mother and I just know he has to be alive somewhere—maybe a prisoner so he couldn't come home to us."

The prince put his arm around Raymond's shoulder. "Annabella, I'm trying to persuade Raymond to come live with us. His mother is ill and that is why Raymond was sent to live with his uncle. But surely she would not want him to live alone, don't you agree?"

Annabella was delighted. *"You'll like living with us, Raymond. Father is becoming quite a good cook and he can tell you anything you want to know about birds and trees."*

Prince Kareem thanked his daughter and then added, *"Furthermore, I could use your help in the garden, Raymond, and I'm thinking of building a stone wall. You'd be doing us a big favor if you moved in."*

"In that case," Raymond said, *"I'll gladly come to live here. You're all very nice to me. But, Magpie, I need your help for something very hard, something I must do right now."* The boy's excitement grew as he spoke. *"Will you take me to that place you told of in your dragon story, the land of the six mountains? I've seen it twice in my dreams. Is it a real place?"*

Magpie was surprised. *"There is such a region,"* he said. *"It lies between the Silver Sea and the Great Desert. The prince and Annabella and I were there just a month ago on our way to the Kingdom of Tall Pines. Did you really dream about it?"*

There was a sudden hush as everyone listened to Raymond. *"In my dreams,"* he began, *"one mountain is dark and gray, not bright like the others. And on that mountain, in the shadows, is a man who reminds me of my father. He seems to be in a cage of some sort and there are creatures with long tails watching him."*

Annabella jumped up. *"The dragons, Magpie! Oh, Raymond, the orange flower people told us all about those dragons. They called them the lost dragons!"*

There was a stirring and fluttering in Magpie's wings that he always felt before a new adventure, though he tried to remain calm. *"I don't know if such dreams as you had are real once we are awake. However, if you will let us borrow your carriage, Prince Kareem, I will travel with Raymond to the six mountains, which may in fact be seven in number."*

Prince Kareem frowned and stroked his chin. "Hmm. Can you drive a carriage, my boy?" he asked doubtfully.

"Oh, yes," Raymond replied eagerly. "My uncle taught me how to handle the horses, sir. I did all the driving for him."

The prince looked at Raymond without saying anything. And then he smiled and shook the boy's hand. "Well, then, it's settled," he said. "You'd better hurry if you're going to reach the boat on time. We'll pack some sandwiches and you two can be on your way."

Beatrix had been silent all this time, but now she spoke. "Let me come," she urged. "You may need some of my magic, you can never tell."

Annabella joined in. "Oh, Magpie, let Beatrix go with you. Remember how dark and scary that mountain looked? And what if the lost dragons really do live there? Beatrix's little brown moth and her blueberry bush might come in handy."

It was agreed that Beatrix would go. However, before the adventurers set out on their way, Raymond excused himself and ran to the cave. He put the tins of meat and the apples into his knapsack and returned quickly to the cottage. Then he told everyone about the bad thing he had done on the ship.

"I stole food," he said sadly. "I had nothing to eat when I snuck on board so I took six tins of meat and some cheese and bread. Well, the cheese and bread are gone but I never opened the tins. Every time I looked at them I felt terrible about being a thief. Now I can return them and maybe the captain will accept these apples in exchange for what I ate."

They were all proud of Raymond. "You are a brave boy," said Magpie. "It's not easy to admit wrongdoing. Well, this is a good way to begin our journey, don't you think so, Beatrix?"

The young witch could not decide if she agreed with Magpie so she smiled at Raymond and changed the subject. "By the way, what do we call your father when we find him?" she asked.

Raymond beamed with pleasure as he spoke his father's name for the first time with his new friends. "Corporal Thomas of the Royal Guard! That's what you can call him."

Several fifth graders inform me at the start that my plan might work but not without difficulty. "It would take a lot of getting used to," says a girl named Rachel, "but it could happen. Right now there's a lot of saying no but if you kept at it a long time you could get it into your brain to say yes."

"Sometimes you don't want to say yes," another girl protests. "Like if I'm playing catch with my dad in the park and a kid is walking home from school and wants to play, my dad might say no, because it doesn't feel right."

"It's a private time with you and your dad," I suggest.

"Right. And sometimes you have times like that with your friends."

"No one would argue about the privacy of those occasions," I say. "But does the classroom qualify as private or public?"

A boy answers. "If he or she is your good friend you can always invite them to your house. So, no, this isn't a private place. It's probably a good rule but it would take years to get used to. You really do have to start in kindergarten. I can still remember kids telling me to go away in kindergarten. I remember a lot of things that happened in school when I was young, most of it not good."

"Wait a minute," the boy next to him says. "In your whole life you're not going to go through life never being excluded. So you may as well learn it now. Kids are going to get in the habit of thinking they're not going to be excluded so much and it isn't true."

"Maybe our classrooms can be nicer than the outside world," I say.

"But this way you won't get down on yourself when you do get excluded," he insists.

"Okay, but, as a teacher, here's what troubles me. Too often it's the same children, year after year, who bear the burden of rejection. They're made to feel like strangers."

"Well," a girl says, "the rule could work in kindergarten because rules are a big thing then. My little sister *likes* rules. But when you get older, some people really don't care. You're a little meaner."

Rachel shakes her head. "I still think if you get in the habit it could work. Like buckling your seat belt." Everyone laughs. "I mean it, really. My parents never made a big thing of that when my big brother was little so he argues about it, but me and my little brother do it before we think about it."

"I agree with Rachel," another girl says. "People can be trained to be nice or to fight. Or both ways, like us."

The children settle back on their pillows and begin swapping stories of early rejections, bittersweet tales, and no one, I notice, relates an incident in which he or she is the one doing the rejecting.

"When I was in kindergarten," a boy recalls, "the girls didn't want me in the doll corner but I really wanted to play in there. I felt really hurt. I don't know if they didn't want any boy or just me. 'No boys! No boys!' It was really weird."

The children have become very serious. They don't laugh at their classmate's memories of the doll corner, but it is an awkward moment. "By the way," I say, "you're the first grade level that thinks the plan might work. The way it's been going, as I move to each higher grade, more children think the plan is fair but also that it won't work. The general feeling is friendship comes before fairness, and the plan is seen as an intrusion into friendship."

A large black boy raises his hand. "Remember me? I came to your room to take your kids to music that time you couldn't do it? Anyway, you were finishing up a discussion. This one kid wanted to be G.I. Joe and the other two boys said he had to be a bad guy so he sat in his cubby and didn't want to play."

"Oh, yes, that was probably Angelo. Or maybe Nelson. Was he white or black?"

"White."

"Then it was Nelson. His feelings were terribly hurt. I guess it wouldn't happen that way in fifth grade."

"Yeah, but it hurts more if the teacher forces people to play with you."

"He's right!" someone calls out. "Last year, one time some guys wouldn't let me play and the teacher came up and told them they had to because they were letting someone else play instead of me and, boy, was it ever uncomfortable standing there, listening to my friends argue with the teacher about letting me play."

"Your friends? They were your friends?"

"Well, yeah, friends will do that. Anyway, I started to play and we got into a fight, and then they didn't talk to me for a few days."

"That does happen," a boy agrees. "Look, if someone comes up to you and they're not especially your friend, and they say can I be your partner, you say no, I already picked someone else when really you didn't. Then you go to a friend and pick him."

"Does the first one know?" I ask.

"No . . . sometimes. Well, yes, they really do. You just pretend you don't. No one makes such a big scene as the G.I. Joe kid."

A curly-haired boy across the rug has had his hand up for a while. "Can I ask you a question, Mrs. Paley? Did you make up this rule, 'You can't say you can't play'?"

His question takes me by surprise and I laugh. "Well, no, I didn't make it up, only the words themselves. The idea is very old, as old as the civilized world. You'll find it in the Bible: 'The stranger that sojourneth with you shall be unto you as the homeborn among you . . .'"

I complete the verse from Leviticus in a room that has grown quiet. The children seem intimidated by my response. "When I first read these lines," I continue, "I didn't think they applied to me. It's not something you can figure out right away."

The time has come for me to leave but I see that the children are still puzzled. "You see, lately, I've come to understand that although we all begin school as strangers, some children never learn to feel at home, to feel they really belong. They are not made welcome enough."

Before school the next morning, Ruthie, the fourth grader who said girls do the most rejecting, comes into my classroom. "How's the rule working?" she asks. When I tell her that the children seem to take the rule for granted already, she nods and smiles. "I knew they would. When I was in kindergarten I would have loved that rule. To tell you the truth, I could use it right now. By the way, where exactly does the rule come from?"

"A fifth grade boy asked me the same question, Ruthie. I've adapted it from the Bible. 'The stranger that sojourneth with you shall be unto you as the homeborn . . .'"

Ruthie's face lights up and she jumps to her feet. "Oh, I know that! I know that! It's in our prayer book! 'For you were strangers in the land of Egypt'!" She sits down abruptly, flushed, and stares at me as if the subject, for her, has found its context.

The captain thanked Raymond kindly for the returned tins of meat and accepted the bag of apples as payment for the other stolen food. "But promise me you'll never be a stowaway again, young man," he said sternly. "It is absolutely against the laws of the sea." When Raymond told him where he and his companions were going, the

captain looked worried. *"Be careful, my boy. It's a fine thing to search for your father, but this may be a dangerous place to enter."*

Raymond grew thoughtful. *"Then we'd better get there fast,"* he replied, looking around for Magpie and Beatrix. They were at the ship's railing, in conversation with the captain's first mate, who also issued some warnings.

"That mountain is covered with thorn bushes and loose rocks," he was saying. *"You should wait until morning to begin your climb."*

However, Raymond could not bear the thought of a delay. As soon as they drove the carriage off the boat, Raymond lost no time in bringing the horses to a gallop. He was determined to reach the mountain before dark, but no matter how they raced, the sun sank even faster. By the time the shadowy form of the mountains rose up before them there was only the light of the moon to show them the path.

"I want to start right now!" Raymond insisted, as he tied up the horses. *"If we wait until morning, there's more of a chance we'll be discovered."* Magpie and Beatrix could see that Raymond was too excited to wait. He pulled down his hat so the moon would not shine on his pale face, and Beatrix turned herself into a moth. Then the three friends entered the fog that surrounded the hidden mountain.

The climb was even harder than the ship's mate had predicted. Every few feet, Raymond slipped on the wet rocks; for each step forward it seemed he took two back. Each time he grabbed for something firm to hold on to, his hands were stabbed by sharp thorns, but he continued to climb higher and higher. Suddenly he called out in a loud whisper, *"Look up there, Magpie! See that dark shape? Isn't that a man?"*

Magpie landed on the narrow ledge above and Beatrix changed

back into her own form so she could help Raymond pull himself up. At one point he almost lost his grip, but Beatrix grabbed both his hands and tugged with all her might. "I'm coming, father, I'm coming!" he cried under his breath as he felt solid ground beneath his feet and began to run.

When Raymond reached the dark form he burst into tears. "Oh, Magpie, it's just a pile of rocks. It's not a man at all. Only rocks and bushes." The boy threw down his hat and wept with disappointment. "I was so sure my father would be here. Why was he in my dreams if we were not to find him here?"

The saddened comrades sat silently for a long time. Then Magpie said softly, "I myself was lost, Raymond, while still in my shell. Beatrix found me and became my friend. So, you see, for every loss there is a finder. And since we can never know where the finding will take place, we must keep up our spirits."

Beatrix was eager to go on. She changed back into a moth and flew off to investigate the other side of the ledge. Almost at once, her hoarse whisper came through the thick fog. "Psst! Come here! Now!" It sounded as if Beatrix was afraid to breathe.

Raymond moved quickly, paying no attention to the thorns that tore at his clothing. He rushed around the ledge and came to an abrupt halt against Magpie. All three stared in amazement. There lay a herd of sleeping dragons, so closely intertwined that they resembled a giant beast encircled by its own tail. Rumbles and snorts and low growls traveled from dragon to dragon and tiny sparks of fire flashed along the ground, lighting up the scene.

At the center of this frightening tribe was a cage, and in it, crouched low, sat a red-haired man, his head resting on his knees. "Papa!"

gasped Raymond, unable to stop himself, and the sound of his cry awakened the sleeping dragons.

I close the storybook but the children lean forward expectantly. Did the chapter end with too much of a cliff-hanger? Perhaps another page or two will bring us to an easier pause in the narrative. I am about to resume reading when Nelson complains, "No fair about Raymond."

"Because of the dragons?"

"Not that. Those kids weren't nice."

Nelson is still thinking about the unhappy classroom episode. The other children respond to his concern: "Yeah, no fair, no fair." It seems I have whisked Raymond away before his school problems are resolved. The idyllic little schoolhouse is not so nice after all, as far as Raymond is concerned.

The children must have known at the time that something was missing from my story. How could a teacher allow a child to run away in tears? "Does Schoolmistress have the new rule?" Lisa had asked, but I avoided her anxiety. "Maybe she hasn't thought enough about it" had been my evasive answer.

More likely, it was I who was not quite ready. Can the rule work in the Kingdom of Tall Pines but not in my class? It is now a moot point. The children want Raymond protected by the rule before he goes off to rescue his father. Furthermore, I take this as a sign that, no matter what backsliding and objections exist, the children, in fact, want equal protection under the law for themselves as well as for Raymond.

"You're right, Nelson," I say. "Raymond might even be too sad to look for his father. Schoolmistress has to do something. After lunch, I'll figure out a way to change the story."

I am not much of a conversationalist as we eat but perhaps the children understand. They bring all their problems and tough-to-open yogurt containers to Sarah. After lunch I begin, making up the story as I go along. "Let's go back to where Prince Kareem invites Raymond to come live with them. This is before Raymond has the dream about his father and asks Magpie to take him to the hidden mountain."

Raymond moved from the lonely cave to the thatched cottage and felt much better because he now lived with people who were good to him.

However, at school, except for Annabella and Alexandra, he still had no friends. Everyone already had made friends and they didn't want to be bothered getting to know Raymond. They kept telling him they would play with him later but they never did.

One day the children were playing kickball, a game Raymond hadn't played before. It's hard to learn things when you're running away and living alone in the woods. Raymond asked the children if he could play.

"Sure you can," said Annabella.

"No, he can't," Peter argued. "I started the game. We have enough players."

"Then we won't play!" Annabella and Alexandra shouted back.

"Okay, okay, he can play," Peter grumbled, but after a few

minutes, when he saw that Raymond was letting all the balls get by him, he changed his mind.

"Oh, I don't care," Raymond told the girls, not wanting to spoil their fun. He walked to the vegetable patch and began pulling weeds next to Schoolmistress.

"I saw what happened, Raymond," she said. "It's not your fault. We need to have a talk with everyone before we go home."

Schoolmistress called the class together after their meal and began a story. "Once upon a time a mother kangaroo and her baby moved to our forest. When they arrived they found that the pine nuts were tasty and the grownups were friendly, but the children did not ask the little kangaroo to play. They had never seen a kangaroo before and didn't seem to like the way he jumped on his back legs.

"'We are runners, climbers, slinkers, fliers, and regular hoppers,' they said, 'not back-leg jumpers.' Even little bear, who had once cried when the other bears chased him away, did not remember how it felt to be unwanted.

"'Can we leave this forest, mother, please?' begged the little kangaroo. 'No one will play with me.'

"'I'll play jolly-jump-up with you,' his mother offered kindly.

"'No thanks, mother. I need to play with animals of my own age.' The next day he jumped his highest jump, raced up and back faster than ever, and did his best flip-flop, but the others turned away, playing their own games. Baby kangaroo sat under a pine tree and cried.

"Then, one by one, the animals came over. 'What's the matter?' asked little bear.

"'Did you get hurt?' little squirrel wondered. The animals crowded around, closer than they'd ever been before, and they noticed that little kangaroo cried the same way they did when they were sad.

"He dried his eyes. 'I have no one to play with,' he told them.

"'Come on, then,' they said. 'Play with us right now. Do you want to be a treasure hunter or treasure hider?' Now little kangaroo was happy, but, later, when he told his mother about it, she wondered why the animals waited until he cried to let him play."

When Schoolmistress ended her story, she asked, "Do any of you know someone who might be lonely? Someone in this class?"

Annabella and Alexandra looked at Raymond, but Peter said, "We're all friends here. No one is lonely."

Raymond could stand it no longer. "Me! I'm the one she means. You and the others never ask me to play!"

Peter was surprised. "But you have Annabella and Alexandra to play with."

"Raymond *is* our friend," Alexandra replied, "but he needs more friends. You're always leaving him out."

Peter objected. "How about you, Alexandra? Since Annabella moved here, she's the only one you play with. And Raymond. Yesterday I wanted to be in your dragon game and you said you had enough dragons."

Schoolmistress smiled. "We all feel sad if we're told we can't play. We need a rule to help us remember."

"I don't need a rule," Peter said quickly. "I'll remember the kangaroo story."

But Schoolmistress shook her head. "Stories are not enough," she told the Olders and the Youngers, while she printed in large letters on the blackboard YOU CAN'T SAY YOU CAN'T PLAY.

I can tell that the children are pleased as they line up for recess. A satisfying balance has been achieved between fact and fiction. Schoolmistress is right: Story is never enough, nor is talk. We must be told, when we are young, what rules to live by. The grownups must tell the children early in life so that myth and morality proclaim the same message while the children are still listening.

"Tomorrow we'll return to the hidden mountain," I remind the children. "Do you remember where we left off?"

"The dragons wake up!" everyone calls out.

"Yes, and Raymond is not afraid," I add, noticing Angelo at my side.

"Now those guys is his friends, right?" he asks, but before I can reply he runs to the front of the line and stands next to Charlie.

The sleepy dragons stepped on one another in confusion, turning their heads back and forth from the red-haired boy to the man in the cage,

as if wondering how the second member of this fiery-headed species could suddenly appear. Magpie whispered to Raymond from the shadows, "Don't be afraid. They haven't seen Beatrix or me. We'll think of a plan."

But Raymond was not afraid. He tried to push through the circle of dragons, then stopped short when his father spoke. "This is my son, Raymond, summoned here from the land of the sun. Does he look dangerous? Of course not! Come now, my friends, I promise you a world of warm sunlight and good food if you'll follow us through the fog."

The dragons moaned when they heard the words "through the fog." They trembled in fear and began to chant, "Spirit of fog, spirit of fire, save us from the funeral pyre!"

Then one of the dragons lifted Raymond gently and put him into the cage with his father. "Corporal of Fire, we welcome your son," he said. Another dragon breathed fire into a pile of branches and soon there was a roaring blaze. The dragons crowded around the fire, stretching and warming their great bodies and grunting with pleasure.

Raymond's father took him tenderly into his arms. "Oh, son, what are you doing here?" he asked sadly. "How did you find me? Why aren't you with your mother?"

Raymond's only response to his father's many questions was to cling closer to him and say over and over, "Mama and I knew you were alive—we knew it, we just knew it!"

"Ah, yes, my child, but now the dragons have us both. I never thought I'd be sorry to see you." The man's face was wet with tears.

Raymond peered about cautiously and then whispered, "Papa, I'm not alone. There are two friends hiding in the shadows. Magpie is a bird and Beatrix is a witch, and they are both very clever. I'm certain they can help us escape." Raymond took his father's hands and looked deeply into his eyes. "Tell me, Papa, do the dragons intend to kill us?"

The man laughed. "Kill us? Heavens, no. Keep us. When the dragons saw my red hair, they thought I was a fire spirit sent to protect them. I came looking for lost treasure but instead found these forlorn creatures who are afraid to let me go. They have never seen the sun and believe only in the fog and fire to save them from the unknown terrors on the other side."

Two dragons approached the cage with platters of large mushrooms and brown spongy pancakes in golden sauce. "These are as you like them, Corporal of Fire. Will you have some tea?" Raymond's father thanked the dragons and asked for two cups of broth, which were brought immediately. "These are all different kinds of mushrooms," he explained to his son. "The dragons are wonderful cooks. They know a hundred ways to prepare mushrooms—but, unluckily, only mushrooms. You see, there is little else that grows in the dark. If I could give them something good to eat from the outside, they might become curious enough to chance the fog and take a look beyond."

"How about blueberries?" said a quiet voice from inside the cage. Corporal Thomas jumped in surprise.

"Who said that?" he asked anxiously.

Raymond put a finger to his lips. "Sh, it's Beatrix. She's on your jacket. See the brown moth?" Raymond smiled at his father's puzzlement. "Beatrix, say hello to my father."

The moth remained absolutely still, having no idea whether or not *dragons eat insects.* "Glad to meet you, Corporal Thomas of the Royal Guard," she whispered. Then she added, "What do you think the dragons might do if I made a blueberry bush appear?"

Corporal Thomas studied the moth on his sleeve. "Can you do this, Beatrix? A real blueberry bush? Well, never mind. Anyone who can change into a moth can certainly produce a blueberry bush. The question is, will the taste of their first blueberries have any special effect on the dragons?"

Raymond continued to eat his mushrooms while he thought about moths and magic and Magpie. Then suddenly he shouted, "Magpie, Magpie, come to the Corporal of Fire! There is a blueberry emergency, O Royal Bird of the Fire Spirit. Come quickly, we are in need of a story!"

The older children now stop me in school occasionally to add another dimension to the debate. In the library a fifth grader tells me, "If someone in my class broke your new rule and was sent into the hall, they'd just goof off—they wouldn't care."

Her thought surprises me. "This wouldn't be the sort of rule you'd get punished for breaking," I say. "If you don't follow what the rule requires, then . . . well, you just think about it and talk about it some more. It isn't a matter of punishing someone, it's more a case of protecting someone."

I thank the girl for speaking to me. Her comment points to something I must find a way of explaining to the children. "You can't say you can't play" is not like the rules prohibiting

114 You Can't Say You Can't Play

hitting or destruction of property. Those behaviors are seldom open for discussion. *Thou Shalt Not* is final and sufficient.

Our new rule is different. It gives us a useful perspective from which to view our actions. Why not simply say "Don't be mean"? People do, of course, tell each other this all the time. The new rule, however, examines a specific yet broad example of *meanness* and uses the imagery of play to do so. Since play is the subject children care the most about, its precise words and actions—especially the negative ones—are easily available and carry the greatest meaning.

"Cynthia is being mean to me," Lisa says when we return from the library. Half of her conversations with the teachers seem to begin with this statement. Sarah and I follow up each accusation in detail because Lisa herself is so often unkind to people. And also because words and explanations are so important to her. "I showed her my fanny pouch and she said, 'Who cares? I've got a thousand of those things!'"

"That does sound unfriendly."

"Isn't that the same as against the rule?" she wonders. It is a good question. Do those casual insults imply "and furthermore I don't intend to let you play"? We now have a general standard against which to view the particulars of each event.

We call Cynthia and Mary Louise to our table and Lisa describes the cause of her unhappiness. "That hurt my feelings. And you always tell Mary Louise not to play with me too!"

Patiently, Cynthia tries to explain. "Sometimes I like to play with Lisa and sometimes with Mary Louise and sometimes with Clara even. So I tell Lisa I'll play with her tomorrow."

Cynthia sees nothing wrong with this arrangement; she is dispensing separate but equal opportunities for play.

"That wouldn't seem to fit the rule," I say, pointing to the sign.

"But I *am* playing with them—on different days."

The logic of her position seems to impress the group gathered around us. The children enjoy listening to any analysis of the new rule. I ask them, "What about Cynthia's idea? Is it the same if you play with one different person each day or with everyone together on one day?"

As the children ponder the question, Lisa protests, "But this *was* my day!" Then she stops to think about it and adds, "But anyway, it *is* against the rule," and most of the children nod their heads.

"Cynthia, your plan is complicated, even more so than the rule. The way I see it, your plan almost forces you to tell the one you're playing with *not* to play with someone else."

She is unsure of my reasoning but decides to make amends. "I made a mistake about the fanny pouch, Lisa. See, my grandma just gave me another one so I have too many and so I forgot how many." Lisa is satisfied and so am I. Every time we analyze the logic of the rule we also think about the logic of our behavior.

Later in the day, the roles are reversed. Now Cynthia complains that Lisa is being mean, telling secrets to Mary Louise and Sheila but not to her. Isn't that against the rule? I tell her that I think she's right, that telling secrets does seem to be the same as keeping someone out of a game. We must discuss this with the class. Meanwhile, I have still another incident to examine with Cynthia. "Hiroko came back from the bathroom before, very upset. She said that you and Lisa laughed at her when she was in a stall and said, 'Don't you think Hiroko stinks?'"

"We didn't know she was in there." A moment's pause. "Lisa said it. I only laughed." By now Lisa and Hiroko have joined us and the incident has been reviewed again.

"You both hurt her feelings. It's the same as telling someone 'We don't like you, you're not nice enough to play with.' It's like saying 'Who cares about a fanny pouch?'"

Lisa looks at me primly. "It's not quite the same," she says, but she knows there might be a connection. Hers is a logical mind and she continually looks for opportunities to compare and sort out the wide variety of behaviors that confront her. Only Lisa would have asked, "Who's nicer, me or Beatrix?"

All the children will learn a great deal from these fairly objective examinations of behaviors in light of the new rule. However, Lisa, Cynthia, Charlie, and Ben, who argue most about it, give us the most to talk about. Lisa, in particular, being determined to identify those she dislikes at any given moment, allows us a rich opportunity to think about the ways in which people are made to feel unliked and unwanted. Even more important, Lisa shows us better than anyone else what you do when you *like* someone, permanently or momentarily.

"Pretend we live in a castle," she says to Hiroko the next day, when they are alone in the room. Both girls have brought notes requesting that they remain indoors at recess time. "Just you and me, Hiroko, in a beautiful castle of gold and diamonds."

Hiroko is surprised and delighted. She gingerly steps into the block structure Lisa has begun to assemble. "And pretend we hear a noise and it's the wicked monster. Hurry up, get in," Lisa whispers. "The monster is coming! This castle has no doors so the monster can't get in but we can get out because we're magic."

"Are we the only magic ones?" Hiroko asks.

"Just us. No one else is alive yet. Only us are born. Pretend that."

Jennifer runs into the classroom. "Mrs. Wilson said I could come in," she tells me, and Lisa welcomes her in royal fashion.

"Oh, there comes another magic princess just born out of the shell! Crawl in this invisible door, quick, Jennifer, because there's no doors to this castle so the monster can't catch us."

This might well be the first time Lisa has invited Hiroko or Jennifer to play with her. The fact that no one else is around is not important. These girls are often on Lisa's worst-friend list, which proves my point: It is the *habit* of exclusion that grows strong; the identity of those being excluded is not a major obstacle.

Lisa's castle tempts me into extravagant analogies. The classroom that allows children to evict others from play is like a castle with no doors. Those inside the castle are invested with magical powers and the outsiders are forced into the role of unlovely monsters.

My hidden mountain is the same phenomenon in reverse. Here lies a race of outcast dragons, frightened and fragile, hidden in a fog-bound eternity, afraid to seek their place in the sun. They do not know that the sun belongs to them as surely as to anyone else, and Magpie and Beatrix must find a way to lure them out. So too must Clara be brought out of hiding into the gold and diamond castle, its doors thrown open for all to enter. It will happen. *It is happening.* Because the children are learning that it is far easier to open the doors than to keep people out.

Magpie stepped from the shadows and flew to the cage that now held Raymond as well as his father. "Royal Magpie, at your service, sir!" he trilled in bugle-like tones.

The dragons backed away timidly as Magpie stretched his wings and glared in their direction. Meanwhile, Beatrix hid herself in his feathers and told him all that she had learned of the trouble at hand. Magpie ruffled his tail and lowered his head. "What is your command, O Corporal of Fire?"

Raymond's father returned the bow. "Welcome, Royal Bird," he said. "My son has a most terrible craving for blueberries. Do you have a story to calm him?"

"Indeed I do, sir," Magpie replied and he began immediately. "Once upon a time," he called out, and the dragons moved toward him as if pulled by a magic cord. "Once upon a time," he repeated softly when the dragons had settled at his feet, "there was a flock of royal geese whose task it was to gather the finest blueberries from the four corners of the earth and bring them to the Emperor's table. He would taste a sample from each basket until he found the most perfectly sweetened,

*delightfully juicy blueberry and then he would order his royal cooks
to make a new dessert for his dinner. 'Surprise me,' he always said.
'Bake something no one else has ever eaten.'*

"*Each day there would be a different blueberry pie, tart, or soufflé.
There were cookies and muffins and pastries of every variety. The
desserts became more extravagant and daring as the months went by
until, one day, after taking his first mouthful of a chocolate blueberry
whipped cream angel food seven-layer cake, the Emperor cried out,
'The blueberries are not fresh!'*

"*He fell into a deep sadness, took to his bed, and refused to eat. The
royal birds brought him ever fresher blueberries and the royal cooks
made even fancier desserts but each time the Emperor turned away
and moaned, 'Not fresh enough.'*

"*Then, early one morning, a small royal dragon crept into the
Emperor's room and whispered into his ear. A weak smile appeared
on the royal face as the Emperor rose from his bed and followed the
little dragon into the garden. There stood a patch of blueberry bushes
with their first ripened berries. The Emperor had never seen his
beloved blueberries as they grew on the bush.*

"'*Ah,' he exclaimed, 'a truly fresh berry!' He grabbed handfuls,
stuffing them into his mouth. 'Fresh blueberries!' he sang out, danc-
ing around the bushes. 'Royal birds! Royal cooks!' he shouted. 'From
now on, no one but my royal dragon may bring me blueberries!' The
Emperor placed a crown upon the dragon's head, sat him at the royal
table, and they lived happily ever after.*"

*Magpie bowed low when the story was over. Instantly, the little brown
moth at his side turned back into Beatrix the witch. She blinked three
times and a blueberry bush appeared. The dragons, of course, were*

astonished. They sniffed the bush and then tasted the strange food, licking their lips excitedly, plucking berries rapidly until the bush was bare. Beatrix blinked three times again and another bush appeared, farther away. When the dragons had devoured all of those berries, another bush sprang up at the edge of the fog that surrounded the mountain, then another a few feet into the fog, then deeper into the darkness until suddenly the dragons emerged into the sunlight. They squinted up at the bright blue sky and warm yellow sun, unbelieving.

Beatrix ran back to release Raymond and his father, who quickly joined the dragons. "Where are we?" the dragons asked, and the corporal pointed to the six mountains bathed in sunlight.

"In the world, my friends, in the beautiful world," he said. "Everything you need is there and always has been there, waiting for you to come out of the fog."

The dragons walked around slowly at first, then began to leap about, chasing one another up and down the mountainside. "Go easy now," called Raymond's father. "There is time to discover your new world, day by day. And we must now return to our home, which is far away from here."

When the dragons heard this, they ran to the corporal. "Stay with us, please!" they begged, but he waved goodbye.

"I'm sorry. I cannot remain any longer. And you no longer need magic spirits to protect you."

Magpie flew to the corporal's shoulder. "Good dragons," he said. "I have a favor to ask. You will one day meet a group of tiny people dressed in orange cactus flowers. Be gentle and kind to them. Tell them you are friends of Magpie and will defend them from the golden eagle." The dragons promised to watch over the orange flower people and Magpie was satisfied.

Beatrix sat waiting in the carriage and, as soon as Raymond and his father climbed aboard, the happy group hurried toward the sea, with Magpie leading the way from high above. After an hour or so, Magpie disappeared into the clouds. He was on his way to bring the news of the rescue to Prince Kareem, Annabella, and Alexandra.

Lisa is learning to adjust to the rule. She sends unwanted characters to live in the woods if she can get away with it, but she reorganizes quickly when her veto is overridden. She is quite remarkable, I think. She asked me recently, "At the end of the talking do we have to do it, or can we keep talking?" It was hard not to laugh. "Yes, after the talking, we *must* do it," I replied. She nodded, taking in the information.

Clara has been one of the last to understand the procedural changes but now she is becoming a party to their workings. She comes upon Lisa and Cynthia as they cover the entrance to their dwelling with scarves and manages to narrate her way in without disrupting the play.

"Pretend we're newborn baby princess mousies," Lisa says to Cynthia.

"And pretend I'm a girl kitty that is lost and I see you," Clara offers hopefully.

"Then you find your sister, Clara, in a different woods and you run away . . ."

"No," Clara says firmly. "Me and my sister see a trail of

cheese and it's your cheese and we come to live in your mousie house."

"But, see, we're all running away," Lisa informs the new players. "Then we see the gold and then we find a haunted house." Lisa remains in charge. She can continue to feel she is in charge because the children welcome her leadership as long as she doesn't keep them outside the castle doors.

The fourth grader who wondered if getting rid of owners and bosses would solve the enigma of exclusionary behavior makes a good point. Children with appealing ideas will always have followers, but the word "boss" creates problems. Another designation is needed. Words do make a difference. Next year, when "You can't say you can't play" will not be a new rule, but simply *the* rule, it will be interesting to see if "boss" and "owner" disappear. And, if they do, what will be invented to take their place?

The play goes so well now that we are unprepared for a new issue that arises, one that confounds the teachers and disturbs the children. Nearly two weeks after "You can't say you can't play" has gone into effect, a simple and logical expansion of the rule to cover the logistics of storytelling and story acting creates a near revolution.

How could I have known that the stories the children dictate for us to act out are even more private and intimate in design and function than play itself? Or is it that these stories are now one of the few places left in which a child can truly be the boss?

The situation comes to a head at Cynthia's birthday party,

in front of her parents, when Lisa explodes in anger. "No fair! I hate you!" she wails. "You promised me!"

Cynthia darts a worried glance at her parents as she defends herself. "No, I didn't promise. I said maybe."

Lisa is inconsolable. She bursts into tears and sits in the center of the rug howling as if in pain. Cynthia's parents are confused and embarrassed. "What's wrong, Cynthia?" her mother asks.

"She's mad at me because I didn't pick her to be in my story." Cynthia herself is on the verge of tears. "I didn't promise, mommy, I said maybe because she was bothering me so much when I was telling the story to Mrs. Paley."

"Couldn't you let Lisa be something?" Cynthia's father asks softly.

"But she didn't let me be in hers!"

"Why not?"

"Because she thinks I like Mary Louise better."

"Oh."

The party has come to a halt. Our method of allowing the author to choose the actors has never seemed entirely fair to me and now we can no longer avoid a careful study of the matter. But, for the present, the two girls must be helped out of their trap.

"Let Lisa be a sister, okay?" I whisper to Cynthia. "Just so the party won't be spoiled. Later we'll have a good talk about it." Cynthia agrees instantly, Lisa stops crying, and the grown-ups are relieved.

However, the nature of the confusion is suddenly clear: The classroom "bill of rights" obviously does not cover story acting.

The author owns all production rights. Though we have, in theory at least, rid ourselves of exclusivity in play, children can still reject one another when their stories are performed. Lisa's tantrum at the birthday party has sent up a distress signal, much as Clara's tearful treks to her cubby had done when playtime was dominated by the boss system.

The following day, I bring my concerns to our discussion group.

Teacher: Mrs. Wilson and I think we need a new way to choose actors for story acting. Some people keep raising their hands and they're never picked—unless the teachers insist.

Hiroko: Mary Louise is always the big sister. I never get to be.

Nelson: I never get to be a turtle.

Teacher: We could solve these problems easily by just going around the rug, giving everyone a chance, one by one.

Charlie: But if it was my story it wouldn't be fair because I know who I want. It's already inside my mind.

Teacher: You always choose the same boys, Charlie.

Angelo: Never me he doesn't.

Waka: But then I can't say I'm sorry! When I have a fight, a argument, something bad when we're playing, then I say I'm sorry and I say you can be in my story.

Karl: Yeah, I even picked Nelson for my story because first I said he couldn't play and then I said he could be in my story.

Teacher: I'm beginning to understand. My new idea would keep you from doing these special favors for people. But, of course, now that everyone is allowed to play . . .

Lisa: I like to *pick* people. I know who I want. What's the use of telling a story?

Teacher: Lisa, a long time ago you said "What's the use of playing?" if you couldn't choose only the people you wanted. But your play is better than ever. The same thing will happen in story acting.

Cynthia: No it won't. Because maybe I'm telling a story that only certain people are in. Like sometimes it's Lisa and I know it has to be Lisa.

Teacher: But at your party it *wasn't* Lisa and she was hurt. If we'd been in the habit of going around, taking turns, she would have known she has to wait until it's her turn.

Clara: Sometimes I want only Lisa in my story.

Charlie: It's not fair because it's *my* story.

Ben: Yeah, it's my notebook. I should be the one to say.

Smita: It *is* fair because I hold my hand high and everyone always picks Lisa and Mary Louise and not me.

Lisa: Then I'll promise Smita, okay? How about if I promise a different person every Monday? And on the other days I just pick who I want.

Teacher: I know it's hard to make changes. You don't know in advance if you'll like a new way of doing things. Even the older children are afraid. But look, you've made the other new rule work. Everyone spends more time playing and plays with more people.

Jennifer: I don't want people I don't like in my story.

Teacher: I understand, really I do. Perhaps I brought this matter up too quickly, but I don't see how we can say yes in play and no in story acting. We really have to try this out. After a while, if we don't see a lot of good things happening, we'll change back.

Lisa: Then I'm not doing any more stories!

Charlie: Me neither.

Lisa and Charlie hold out for two days and then resume their storytelling as if nothing had gone amiss. Oddly enough, when they return to the story table, each one tells a Magpie story.

This is Charlie's: "Once upon a time there was three dragons and Magpie. The little orange people lived on a mountain. They said to the dragons, 'Go up and breathe fire on the orange pinkleberries.' And then Beatrix came with Magpie and everyone ate the pinkleberries."

Lisa listens to Charlie's story and follows suit: "Once upon a time Beatrix was eating all the poppy seed berries and she got sick with chicken pox. Then the dragons told Annabella to get her father to cure Beatrix. And her father said tell Beatrix never again to eat those poison berries. And Beatrix was cured forever and she decided to go and live with the orange flower people and they called her Princess Beatrix."

Their stories surprise me. Why, after such fierce disapproval of the change in story acting, do Lisa and Charlie come back into the mainstream with a Magpie story? Furthermore, they each choose to be an orange flower person, a rather amorphous, unprepossessing role. I soon find out that these events fit into a general pattern of increased experimentation and flexibility that begins to surround the storytelling activity.

First, there is a running accompaniment of rule-making as we try out the new method of choosing actors: If it's your turn to fill a role and you're a girl but it's a boy's part, the author must change the character to a girl; or, if it's your turn, and you'd rather be something else, the author must add a new character; or, if you don't want any role in that story, you must be given a part in the next, and so on. Each suggested change is elaborated into numerous versions, but there remains one inviolate rule: The author has the right to refuse to change the story in any way. That is what most children choose to do.

Now, a new phenomenon appears: Relieved of the responsibility of looking for loopholes in the law, the children have an opposite reaction. If they cannot change the role, then they will accept *any* role. They dare to take on implausible roles, shyly at the start, but after a while with great aplomb, as if accepting the challenge to eliminate their own stereotyped behaviors. Girls take on boys' roles and boys accept girls' roles. Not everyone, to be sure, but enough children are willing to throw off their shackles to make these role reversals acceptable. Those who have never taken roles as bad guys, witches, and monsters are saying yes to such assignments, and the Ninja Turtles are agreeing to be newborn babies.

What is happening? Perhaps, in giving up control of who plays which character, the storytellers are liberating themselves from the demands of peer expectations. Furthermore, the actors, now chosen by chance, not by preference, no longer feel beholden to the author for approval.

"I still don't like the new way," Lisa tells me privately one day. "Cynthia doesn't either and also Mary Louise."

"One thing you did though, Lisa, made Mrs. Wilson and me very happy."

"I did?"

"Remember when it was Angelo's turn and you needed a father? You said, 'Good, a boy! I didn't want a girl for a father.' You were happy to have Angelo in your story. Do you know why that pleased us so much?"

"Because you like Angelo?"

"That's true, and now he feels you like him also. A long time ago you refused to be his partner in the M & M counting game."

Lisa recalls the incident immediately. "But I gave him all the M & M's and I didn't say anything bad."

"I know, Lisa, you even pretended you weren't hungry. But now, when you saw he was going to be the father in your mousie story, you smiled at him." I stroke her cheek gently and she throws her arms up and hugs me. "Lisa, I really do think the new way is working well."

"How do you know?"

"For one thing, I think the stories are better, although that's hard to prove. Something else is easier to prove, and we've kept track: Everyone has more turns and no one is left out. Besides, we're nicer to each other at story time. No one is telling someone else 'You can't be in my story.'"

Later, before we begin to act out the day's stories, I repeat my reasons for liking the new way of choosing actors, then add the most important argument of all: "We know how much some of you would still like to pick your own actors. But if we're going to learn to stop rejecting people in school we can't have one activity in which children are still told they are not wanted."

I am fairly certain this makes sense to the children but I add an extra bit of support. "By the way, you children are really being good sports. Now that the authors are no longer saying no to you, more of you are saying yes to the authors. Remember when some of you would refuse to be in a person's story if he or she had done something you didn't like? I don't see that any more."

The children, of course, cannot possibly be aware of all the changes Sarah and I have been watching. I feel a tinge of regret that next year's class will begin the school year with "You can't say you can't play" as a given. It must be so, for I can never go back to the old ways. Yet the real excitement has been in the process of discovery.

However, the concept of open access, I suspect, can never be taken for granted, but must in fact be rediscovered each year by each new group. "You can't say you can't play" is apparently not as natural a law as, for example, "I say you can't play."

That being the case, we have our work cut out for us, in every grade, if we are to prepare our children to live and work comfortably with the strangers that sojourneth among them.

And should it happen that one day our children themselves are the strangers, let them know that a full share of the sun is rightfully theirs.

It seemed to Beatrix that Raymond and his father would never stop talking. Their questions and stories kept pace with the swiftly moving horses' hooves. Beatrix made herself as quiet as could be until she heard the corporal speak of going directly to Raymond's mother. Then she felt she must interrupt. "Corporal," she asked timidly, "won't you even stay a bit to see the prince?"

"Oh, but of course, Beatrix," he replied. "My wife would not forgive me if I didn't thank him and the girls for their kindnesses to Raymond. Besides, the horses need rest and I'll want the prince's permission if we are to use them again."

Magpie was waiting at the dock. "It's coming! Do you hear the bells?" he called, giving several shrill whistles to signal the approaching schooner.

The moment the travelers came aboard, the captain rushed up to the corporal. "So it was you the boy was looking for!" he said. "Now I do remember. Didn't you ride with me two or three years ago? Something about a treasure hunt?"

Corporal Thomas clasped the captain's hand. "It was four years ago, sir," he replied. "My son was but a lad of six when I went away to war. It wasn't a long war, but on the way home I found a treasure map, and the idea of coming home a rich man took hold of me. I could think of nothing else." He put his arm around Raymond and shook his head sadly. "Forgive me, son. What a foolish man your father has been."

As they neared the shore, Raymond began to wave his arms. "Look, papa! Look what Annabella and Alexandra have made for you!" The girls were holding up a long banner on which they had printed WELCOME HOME CORPORAL THOMAS.

"Humph," grumbled Beatrix. "How about the rest of us? Don't we get welcomed home?" A few moments later, her complaint was answered. Prince Kareem lifted another sign, the paint still wet. It said CONGRATULATIONS BEATRIX, RAYMOND, AND MAGPIE. *"There, you see? The prince has put my name first!"*

Magpie could not help laughing at her. "Oh, Beatrix, you are really quite funny, you know. Well, never mind, you deserve to be first. Your blueberry bushes were the most important part of the rescue." The young witch beamed with pleasure.

Suddenly, Raymond's father grew quiet, staring ahead at the tall pines. "Can it be?" he said under his breath. "Is it possible?" He continued to examine the shoreline and trees with puzzlement. When the ship dropped anchor, he turned to his son and stated firmly, "I've been here before." Then, after being introduced to Prince Kareem and the princesses, he began a strange story.

"I have passed through this forest, not once, but twice, without knowing its name." He looked at his startled audience, then sat down on a large rock. "On my way home from the wars," he continued, "I discovered an old rolled-up map in the hollow of a tree. The reason I was certain it would lead me to a fortune is that right next to it, on

the ground, was a magpie egg. The magpie is thought to bring good luck, you know. The little egg lay alone in a partly overturned nest, blown away in a storm, I would guess. There was no use in trying to put the nest back, for it was much too damaged and, besides, the mother was nowhere to be seen. So, figuring that the magpie would be my lucky charm, I decided to take it with me and keep it warm until it hatched."

Magpie had begun to fly from branch to branch, his feathers tingling all over. Everyone's eyes followed him until the corporal resumed his tale. "I placed the egg in my pocket and turned it carefully as I walked along, feeling a slight movement inside the egg. The magpie was alive! My mind was entirely on the magpie and the treasure as I entered the forest. And then, somehow, I lost the egg. Perhaps it rolled out of my pocket when I lay down to rest. Later, when I realized the egg was gone, I ran back and searched everywhere but couldn't find the egg. I've always thought this was the reason for my bad luck."

Magpie could not remain silent any longer. "Sir," he said in a shaky voice, "I am honored to inform you that it was my life you saved. Four years ago, immediately after you lost me in this forest, Beatrix found me and raised me as her own child. This is truly an amazing coincidence!"

The prince had been quiet and thoughtful while he listened to all these revelations. Now he laughed with great joy. "Magpie," he said, "remember what I told you long ago when we first met? I believe in magical forces. You were sent to bring my daughter and me to the Kingdom of Tall Pines and then to save little Prince Orange Flower. Next Raymond appeared. Perhaps he had to come here in order to dream of the hidden mountain. Then you and he and Beatrix found Corporal Thomas and, lo and behold, he turns out to be the one who found you in the first place."

The prince put his hands on the corporal's arm. "To me, every sign points to one certainty, sir. These strange events have led us all here together. I really believe that you and your family should make your home in this kingdom."

Raymond embraced his father. "Papa, could we? Would Mama like the idea?"

The corporal smiled at his son. "We shall ask her. However, the first thing we must do is help her get well. That is now our most important task."

"I agree," said Prince Kareem. "Our piney air is splendid for any illness. And you are most welcome to stay with Annabella and me until you are settled. That is, if you decide to come." Raymond and his father looked at each other and knew they would soon return to the Kingdom of Tall Pines.

I decide to revisit the third grade class to see how the two rejected children, Shirley and John, are doing.

"Since I first came in," I ask the class, "have any of you changed your minds? Can the plan work?"

There is a chorus of no's. "With some people it could work," a boy says, "but not in this class."

Shirley speaks up. "We're starting it to work a little better." She is about to add something, but hesitates.

"You're seeing some changes, Shirley?" I ask.

"The plan works with certain people," says the girl next to her. "About half. But the point is, those people are afraid the others won't like them anymore if they say yes to certain people."

"I see. But which is the more powerful idea, yes or no? Like or dislike?"

"Disliking is much more powerful," John says, but Shirley disagrees.

"I think like is, because one day we sat down and thought a while and we decided to have a party in the playground every two Fridays and anybody, it doesn't matter who, can come to the party."

As she talks, I sense something important has happened. "Shirley," I say, "you're saying *we* are having a party. *We.* I don't remember you saying we before."

Shirley looks at me, wide-eyed. We have not crossed the Silver Sea yet, but we may be getting there.